101 THINGS THAT FLY

HEARST BOOKS
New York

An Imprint of Sterling Publishing
387 Park Avenue South
New York, NY 10016

ISBN 978-1-61837-128-7

Distributed in Canada by Sterling Publishing
c/o Canadian Manda Group, 165 Dufferin Street
Toronto, Ontario, Canada M6K 3H6

Distributed in the United Kingdom by GMC Distribution Services
Castle Place, 166 High Street, Lewes, East Sussex, England BN7 1XU

Distributed in Australia by Capricorn Link (Australia) Pty. Ltd.
P.O. Box 704, Windsor, NSW 2756, Australia

For information about custom editions, special sales, and premium and corporate purchases, please contact Sterling Special Sales at 800-805-5489 or specialsales@sterlingpublishing.com.

Manufactured in China

2 4 6 8 10 9 7 5 3 1

www.sterlingpublishing.com

Popular Mechanics

101 THINGS THAT FLY

PLANES, ROCKETS, WHIRLY-GIGS & MORE!

HEARST BOOKS
New York

CONTENTS

FOREW**O**RD

Nothing screams excitement like toys and rides that go sky high! In our modern-day world of smart phones, tablets, and computer games, it can be easy to forget the joy derived from toys that not only simulate action, but in fact *are* the action. From kites and paper planes to swings and coasters, these flyers color some of our most beloved childhood memories. And they were all the more special if you'd constructed them yourself—not only were they great fun to use; they were also great fun to build.

Enter: *Boy Mechanic's 101 Things That Fly*. Packed with high-flying DIY projects from early issues of *Popular Mechanics*, this book harks back to an era when imagination, craft, and ingenuity ruled. Back in the early twentieth century, building your own entertainment was a source of pride and deeply felt ownership. The projects featured in *101 Things That Fly* reignite that spirit of home craftsmanship, and upon completion they will soar, lift, float, and take passengers on thrilling, unforgettable rides.

Whether you're a kid or a kid at heart, everybody will enjoy a flip through these airborne projects. Prepare for takeoff in Chapter One, where you'll find an assortment of gliding gizmos such as kites, paper planes, and boomerangs. In Chapter Two, toys and games take to the air, from a Jumping Toy Frog and Tiny Acrobat to tossing contests like "Skip Scotch"

and an Indoor Baseball Game to a variety of shooting targets. Great gravity-defying rides commence in Chapter Three, where you'll get an exhilarating lift from swings, seesaws, and merry-go-rounds. Chapter Four soars through the outdoors with projects such as a Water-Coasting Toboggan and Slide, homemade water skis, outdoor gymnasium equipment, and archers' bows and arrows. Finally, in Chapter Five, we've included feats of levitation magic for the amateur trickster— the Flying Thimble and Empty-Glass Lift are two especially clever gags—as well as gravity experiments for the budding scientist.

In keeping with the nostalgic charm of the original *Popular Mechanics* projects, we've left them exactly as they appeared almost one hundred years ago. The toys, games, tools, techniques, and writing style are clearly of another era. So, if venturing to construct these projects, be sure to use only modern tools and techniques and proceed with the utmost caution—ensure that all safety measures have been taken in your workshop, and do not begin any work without the supervision of an adult.

Fortunately, you don't need to build these projects to enjoy them. The reading in itself is an entertaining history lesson that showcases the creativity and gumption of a bygone era—no tools required. Simply flip to the next page and enjoy the flight!

The Editors
Popular Mechanics

101 THINGS THAT FLY

GLIDING GIZMOS

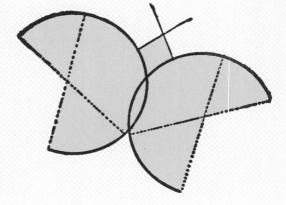

BUTTERFLY KITE

One of the prettiest kites of all is the butterfly kite. To make this, get two thin kite sticks of equal length. Bend each in an arc, tying one end of a strong string to one end of each stick and the other end of the string to a point about 3 in. from the other end of the stick. This leaves one end of each stick free, hooking over the hemisphere described by the thread and the stick. Now tie another thread to each of these free ends and tie the other end of the thread to a point near the other end of the stick, corresponding with the distance from the end at which the first strings were tied on the opposite side. This done, you should have two arched frames, each an exact counterpart of the other in size, curvature, and weight. Now fasten the two frames together so that the arcs will overlap each other, as shown in the sketch. Bind the intersecting points securely with thread.

To make the butterfly's head, secure two heavy broom straws or two short wires, and attach them to the top part of the wing frames near where the sticks intersect, so that the straws or wires will cross. These form the antennae, or the "smellers." Then select the color of paper you want: yellow, brown, blue, white, or any other color. Lay it on a flat surface and place the frame on top of it, holding the frame down securely with a weight. Then with a pair of scissors, cut the paper around the frame, leaving about a ½-in. margin for pasting. Cut slits in the paper about 2 in. apart around the curves and at all angles to keep the paper from wrinkling when it is pasted. Distribute the paste with a small brush and make the overlaps a little more than ¼ in. wide and press them together with a soft cloth. When the kite is dry, decorate it with paint or strips of colored paper in any design you may fancy. The best effects are produced by pasting pieces of colored paper on top of the other paper. Black paper decorations show up to fine advantage when the kite is in flight. Attach the "belly-band" to the curved sticks by punching a hole in the same manner as it is attached to the common hexagonal or coffin-shaped kites. With a tail, your kite is ready to fly.

Boy
Kite

101 THINGS THAT FLY

Another interesting design is the boy kite, which always attracts attention and affords splendid sport for the American youth in springtime. In making a boy kite, it should be remembered that the larger the boy is, the better he will fly. To construct the frame, two straight sticks, say, 3 ½ ft. long, should serve for the legs and body; another straight stick forms the spine and should be about 2 ft. 4 in. long. For the arms, get a fourth straight stick about 3 ft. 3 in. long. Make the frame for the head by bending a light but tough stick in a circle about 7 in. in diameter. Bind it tightly with a strong thread and through its center run the spine. Then tack on the arm stick 3 in. under the circle so that the spinal column crosses the arm stick exactly in the center. Wrap tightly with strong thread and tack on the two sticks that are to serve for the legs and body. The leg sticks should be fastened to the arm stick about 6 in. on either side of the spinal column, and crossed so that the other ends are 3 ft. apart. Tack them and the arm stick together at the point where they intersect. Small hoops and cross stick of the same material as the head frame should be fastened to both extremities of the arm stick and the lower ends

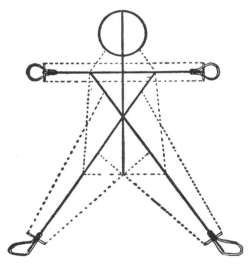

of the leg sticks for the hands and feet. See that both hand frames are exactly alike and exercise equal caution regarding the foot frames; also see that the arm stick is at exact right angles with the spine stick and that the kite joints are all firmly tied and the kite evenly balanced; otherwise, it may be lopsided. Fasten on the strings of the frame, beginning at the neck at equal distances from the spine, as indicated by the dotted lines in the diagram. Extend a string slantingly from the arm stick to the head on both sides of the spinal column, and run all the other strings as shown in the cut, being careful that both sides of the frame correspond in measurements.

To cover the kite, select different colors of paper to suit your taste, and after pasting them together, lay the paper on the floor and, placing the frame on it, cut out the pattern. Leave an edge of ½ in. all around and make a slit in this edge every 6 in. and at each angle; make the slits 2 in. apart around the head. After the kite is pasted and dry, paint the buttons, hair, eyes, hands, feet, etc., as you desire. Arrange the "belly-band" and tail band and attach the kite string in the same manner as in the ordinary coffin-shaped kite.

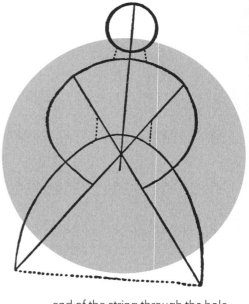

LADY KITE

The "lady kite" is made on the same principle as the boy kite. The frame is made exactly as the boy kite and then "dressed" with tissue paper to represent a girl. Remember the dotted lines represent the strings or thread, and the other lines indicate kite sticks. Be careful with your measurements so that each side of the kite corresponds exactly and is well balanced. Also see that every point where the sticks intersect is firmly tacked and bound.

To cover the kite, first paste together pieces of tissue paper of different colors to suit your taste. The paste should be made of flour and water and boiled. Make the seams or overlaps not quite ⅜ in. wide. Lay the paper on the floor, using weights to hold it down, and place the frame of the kite upon it. Then cut out the paper around the frame, leaving an edge of ½ in. Don't forget to make a slit in the edge every 6 or 7 in. and at each angle. Around the head, the slits are cut 2 in. apart, as in the case of the boy kite. After the kite is dry, paint the paper however your fancy dictates.

To make the breast band, punch holes through the paper, one upon each side of the leg sticks, just above the bottom, and one upon each side of the arm sticks at the shoulders. Run one end of the string through the hole at the bottom of the left limb and tie it to the leg stick; tie the other end at the right shoulder. Fasten one end of another string of the same length at the bottom of the right leg; pass the string up across the first band and tie the other end at the left shoulder. Attach the kite string to the breast band at the point where the two strings intersect. Tie the knot so that you can slide the kite string up or down until it is properly adjusted. The tail band is made by tying a string to the leg sticks at the bottom of the breast band. Let the string hang slack below the skirt and attach the tail to the center. The same general rules apply in attaching the string and tail to the boy kite.

To make the lady look as if dancing and kicking in the clouds— make the feet of stiff pasteboard and allow them to hang loose from the line which forms the bottom of the skirt. The feet will move and sway with each motion of the kite.

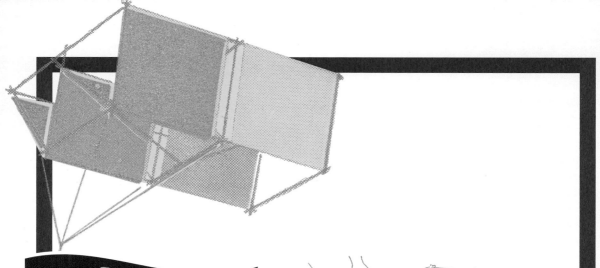

THE W-KITE

The W-Kite, one of the highest fliers and most efficient climbers of all kites, combines the stability of the regular box kite and the strength of the triangular box kite. It flies well without a tail and, in a fair breeze, will "walk" right up to a spot almost directly overhead. It does not pull hard, as does the box, because it adjusts itself constantly. In a fair breeze, it can be fed into the air from the hand and brought back to the hand without ever touching the ground.

The frame is made of any light wood and covered with cellophane. The joints of the frame are tied with string or heavy thread and then coated with shellac or glue. The cellophane cover should not be pulled too tightly, as it may shrink. Where necessary, back the cellophane with a light network of thread tied to the frame. A four-legged bridle is used, the length of the top two legs being about the same as the kite's short struts. The method of attaching the bridle can be seen in the illustration. The size of the kite may be varied, provided the proportions of the parts remain the same as pictured.

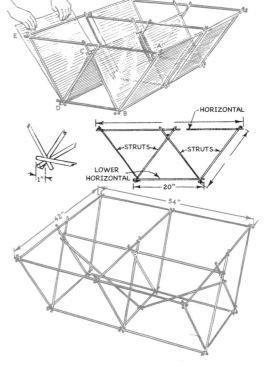

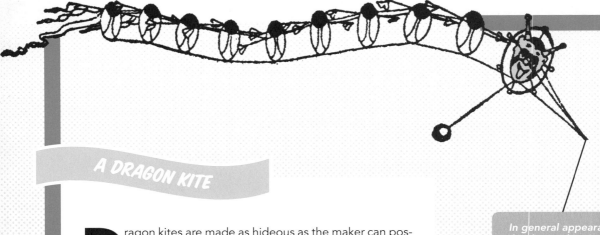

A DRAGON KITE

Dragon kites are made as hideous as the maker can possibly imagine them. Although the one to be considered is no beauty, it is more droll than fierce-looking. In general appearance, the dragon and centipede kites are like huge caterpillars floating about in the air. The kite sometimes twists and the balancer sticks appear to be large, hairy spines. Usually, the tail end swings higher than the head. It is like so many single kites, pulling hard and requiring a strong cord for the line. The individual circular sections may number 20 and if placed 30 in. apart would make a kite about 50 ft. in length, or the number of sections may be more or less to make the kite longer or shorter. The kite will fold up into a very small space, for carrying about or for storage. But care should be taken in folding not to entangle the harness.

THE HEAD

The head requires much more work than any of the other sections. There are two principle rings to this section, as shown in *Figure 1*. The inner ring is the more important, the outer one being added for the protection of the points when alighting. The construction of the framework is shown in *Figure 2*. It is made entirely of bamboo. The bamboo is split into strips, about ³⁄₁₆ in. wide, for the ring A. As the bamboo strips will be much too thick, they must be pared down to less than ¹⁄₁₆ in. The diameter of the ring A is 12 in., and a strip of bamboo to make this ring should be about 38 in. long, so that there will be some end for making a lap joint. The ends of the strip are held securely together by winding them with linen thread. Some boys use strips of rice paper that are about ½ in. wide and torn lengthwise. The rice-paper strips are made wet with paste

In general appearance, the dragon kite is like a huge caterpillar floating about in the air.

The kite-head section, having horns, ears, and revolving eyes, is very hideous.

FIG.1

CONT

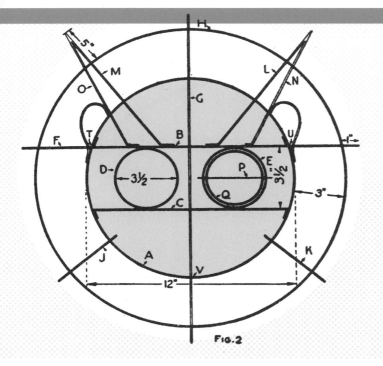

FIG. 2

The framework for the head section is made entirely of bamboo strips lashed at the joints.

before winding them on the joint. When they dry out, the shrinkage will bind the ends securely.

Two crosspieces, of the same weight as the ring stick, are placed 3 ½ in. apart, at equal distances from the center and parallel, as shown in *B* and *C*. The ends of these pieces are turned at a sharp angle and lashed to the inside surface of the ring *A*. To make these bends, heat the bamboo over a candle flame until it will give under pressure, and then bend it. The bamboo will stay in shape after it becomes cold. This method of bending should be remembered, because it is useful in making all kinds of kites. Two small rings, each 3 ½ in. in diameter, are put in between the two parallel pieces, as shown in *D* and *E*. These are for the eyes of the dragon. The rings are lashed to the two crosspieces *B* and *C*. Because the eyes revolve in the rings, they should be made perfectly true. This can be done by shaping the bamboo about a perfectly round cylinder, 3 ½ in. in diameter. To stiffen the whole framework, two pieces of bamboo, ¹⁄₁₆ in. thick, ⅛ in. wide, and 20 in. long, are lashed to the back as shown by *F* and *G*. There is a space of 3 in. between the inner ring *A* and the outer ring *H*, giving the latter a diameter of 18 in. It is made of a bamboo strip, ⅛ in. wide, and should be less than ¹⁄₁₆ in. thick. It may be necessary to make this large ring from two pieces of bamboo to get the length. In such a case, be careful to make a perfect ring with the ends well lashed together. Two short pieces are lashed together to the two rings, as shown in *J* and *K*. The supports for the horns consist of two pieces, ⅛ in. wide and less than ¹⁄₁₆ in. thick, and they are lashed to the upper crosspiece and to both rings, so that the parts *L* and *M* are exactly halfway between the ends of the pieces *F* and *G*, and radiate out from the center of the ring *A*. The other parts, *N* and *O*, point to the center of the eye rings, respectively. The ears are unimportant and may be put on if desired. The rings on the horns and the stick ends may be from ½ to 2 in. in diameter, cut from stiff paper, but if larger, made of bamboo.

Chinese rice paper is the best material for covering, and it should be stretched tightly so that there will be no buckling or bagging places. The only part covered is that inside of the inner ring A, the horns and the ears, leaving the eye rings open. The shades are put on with a brush and watercolors, leaving the face white, or it can be tinted in brilliant colors. Leave the horns white and color the tongue red.

THE EYES

The frame for each eye is made of bamboo, pared down to $\frac{1}{32}$ in. in thickness and formed into a perfect ring, 3 ¼ in. in diameter. Each ring revolves on an axle made of wire passed through the bamboo exactly on the diameter, as shown in P, Figure 3. The wire should be long enough to pass through the socket ring D or E, Figure 2, also, and after the eye ring is in place in the socket ring and the axle adjusted, the latter is fastened to the eye ring with a strip of paper wrapped tightly around the wire and pasted to the bamboo of the ring. A glass bead, placed on the wire axle between

the socket rings D or E and the eye ring Q on each side, keeps them apart and the revolving one from striking the other.

Each side of the eye ring is covered halfway with rice paper, as shown in Figure 4. The part R is on the upper front half, and that shown by S is on the back lower half. Placing the two halves in this manner causes an unequal pressure of the wind on the whole eyepiece, and thus causes it to revolve on the axle. The front upper half of the eyepiece is made black, and the smaller dark portion extending below the darkened half is a round piece of paper placed just between the two halves so that

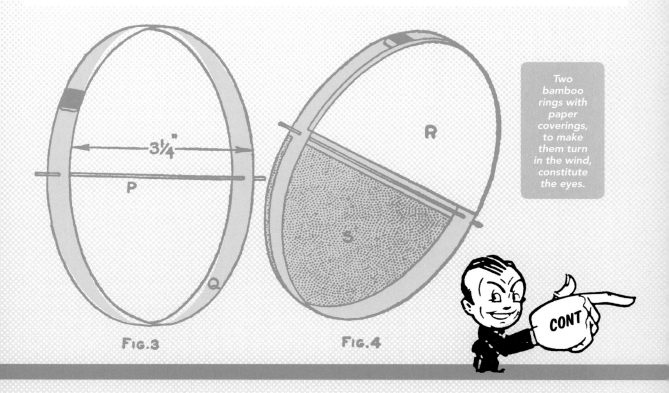

P

3¼"

Q

Fig.3

R

S

Fig.4

Two bamboo rings with paper coverings, to make them turn in the wind, constitute the eyes.

CONT

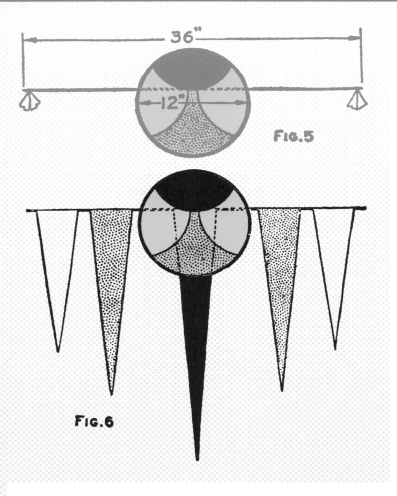

36"

12"

FIG.5

FIG.6

must be made small, light, and well balanced. Small tufts of tissue paper or feathers are attached to the tip ends of the balancer sticks, as shown in *Figure 5*. The cover for the section kite is put on tightly, the same as for the head; the builder can color them as desired. The balancer on the last section should have streamers, as shown in *Figure 6*, for a finish. The streamers are made of light cloth.

THE HARNESS

As previously stated, 20 sections more or less can be used, and the number means so many separate kites which are joined together with three long cords, spacing the sections 30 in. apart. The cords should be as long as the kite from the head to the tail, allowing sufficient extra length for the knots. As such a kite will make a hard pull, the cord used should be six-ply, hard-twisted seine twine. Start by tying the three long cords to the head kite at the points *T*, *U*, and *V*, *Figure 2*. Tie the next section at corresponding places just 30 in. from the head kite. The construction will be much easier if the head kite is fastened to a wall so that each cord may be drawn out to its proper length. Continue the tying until all sections are attached just 30 in. apart. Other spacing can be used, but the distance selected must be uniform throughout the length of the kite. The individual kites, or sections, may vary in

half of it will show on both front and back of the eyepiece. When the eyepiece is given a half turn in its socket, the backside will come to the front and will appear just the same as the other side. Some kite builders add pieces of mirror glass to the eyes, to reflect the light and cause flashes as the eyes revolve in their sockets.

A SECTION KITE

The ring for the section kite is made the same size as the inner ring of the head kite, or in this case 12 in. in diameter. The bamboo for making this ring should be ⅛ in. wide and 1/16 in. thick. The balancer stick, 36 in. long, is located about the same place as the cross stick *F*, as shown in *Figure 2*, and

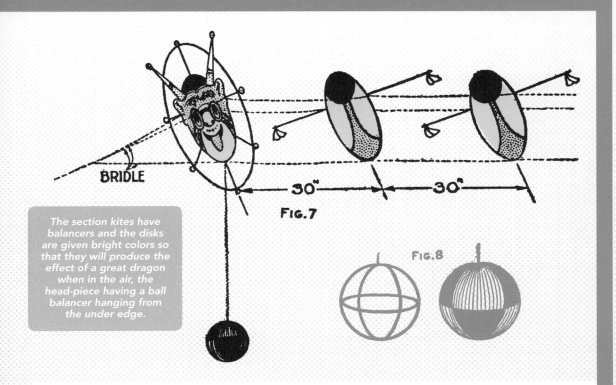

BRIDLE

FIG. 7

FIG. 8

The section kites have balancers and the disks are given bright colors so that they will produce the effect of a great dragon when in the air, the head-piece having a ball balancer hanging from the under edge.

size, or they can all be 9 in. in diameter instead of 12 in., and the balancer sticks 30 in. long instead of 36 in., but a kite of uniform sections is much better and is easier to make. The positions of the sections as they will appear in the kite are shown in *Figure 7*.

THE BRIDLE

The Chinese bridle is usually made of three strings, which are attached to the same points on the head kite as the harness cords, or at *T*, *U*, and *V*. The lower string is longer than the two upper ones so that the

proper inclination will be presented to the breeze. As the head is inclined, all the section kites will also be inclined. Some makers prefer a balancer on the head kite, and in one instance such a balancer was made in the shape of a ball. A ball made of bamboo strips is shown in *Figure 8*, and is attached as shown in *Figure 7*.

FLYING THE KITE

It will be necessary to have a helper, and perhaps two, in starting the kite up because the harness might become entangled. Quite a little run

will be necessary, but when up the kite will make a steady flier and will pull very hard. If the first attempt is unsuccessful, try readjustment of the bridle or a little different position in the breeze, and see that the balancers are not tangled. Quite a number of changes may be worked out on these plans, but it is necessary to bear in mind that the distances between sections must be equal and that the general construction must be maintained.

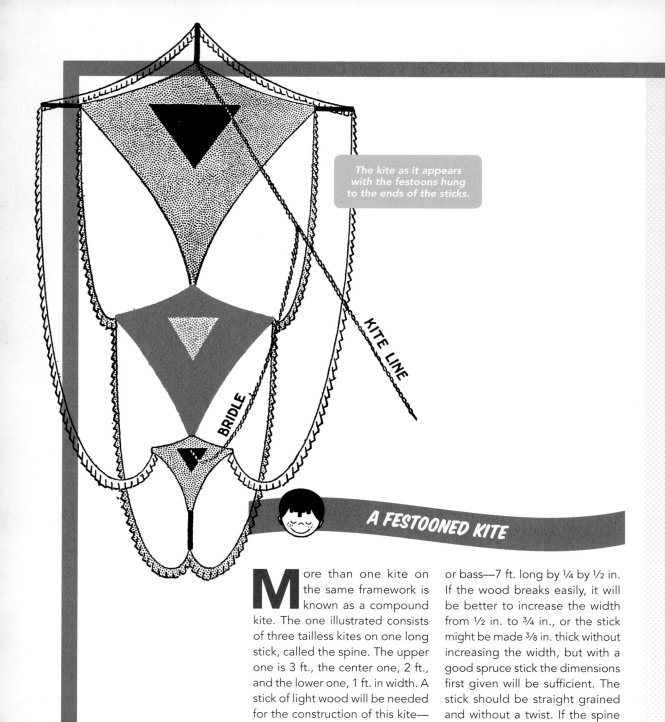

KITE LINE

BRIDLE

A FESTOONED KITE

More than one kite on the same framework is known as a compound kite. The one illustrated consists of three tailless kites on one long stick, called the spine. The upper one is 3 ft., the center one, 2 ft., and the lower one, 1 ft. in width. A stick of light wood will be needed for the construction of this kite—spruce is best, but it may be pine or bass—7 ft. long by ¼ by ½ in. If the wood breaks easily, it will be better to increase the width from ½ in. to ¾ in., or the stick might be made ⅜ in. thick without increasing the width, but with a good spruce stick the dimensions first given will be sufficient. The stick should be straight grained and without a twist. If the spine is twisted, the kites will not lie flat or in a plane with each other. If one is out of true, it will cause the kite to be unsteady in the air. The bow sticks are three, the upper one being 4 ft. long by ¼ by ½ in., the center one, 2 ft. long by ¼ by ⅜ in., and the lower one, 1 ft. long by ¼ by ¼ in. About five sheets of tissue paper will be required, but more may be needed for color combinations. The so-called French tissue paper is much better, as it comes in fine colors and is much stronger than the ordinary tissue. It costs a trifle more, but it pays in making a beautiful kite. The Chinese rice paper is the strongest, but comes only in natural colors.

It will be seen that the kites do not extend to the top and bottom of the spine stick. The first bow stick is placed 13 in. from the top end of the spine, and each of its ends extends 6 in. beyond the kite for fastening the festoons. The bow sticks should be lashed to the spine, not nailed. Wind diagonally around the two sticks, both left and right, then wind between the two, around the other windings. This draws all windings up tightly to prevent slipping.

To string up the upper kite, drill a small hole through the spine 6 in. from the top, at A. Also drill 6 in. from each end of the bow stick, at B and C. If a small drill is not available, notch the stick with a knife or saw to hold the string. Another hole is made in the spine 29 in. from the upper bow stick, or at D. Tie the outline string at A, then pass through the hole at C, then through D, up through B and back to the starting point at A. In tying the last point, draw up the string tightly, but not enough to spring the spine or bow. Measure carefully to see if the distance AC is the same as AB and if CD is equal to BD. If they are not, shift the string until they are equal and wind at all points, as shown in E, to prevent further slipping. Proceed in the same way with the center and lower kite, and it will be ready for the cover.

The cover tissue should be cut about 1 in. larger all around than the surface to be covered, but turn over about half of this allowance. This will give plenty of looseness to the cover. For the fringe festoons, cut strips of tissue paper 2 ½ in. wide, past ½ in. of one long edge over a string, and cut slits with scissors at intervals of 1 in. along the loose edge.

After the fringe has been made, attach it as shown in the illustration. Do not stretch it tightly but give sufficient looseness to make each length form a graceful curve and keep the sides well balanced.

To bend the bows of the upper and center kites, attach a string from end to end of each bow on the back side of the kite and spring in short brace sticks.

Attach the upper end of the bridle at A. The length of the bridle string is 87 in. and the kite line is attached to it 30 in. from A, leaving the lower part from this point to F, where it is tied to the spine, 57 in. long.

The kite should fly without a tail, but if it dodges too much, attach extra streamers to the ends of the bow sticks of the lower kite and to the bottom of the spine.

If good combinations of colors are used, a very beautiful kite will be the result, and one that will fly well.

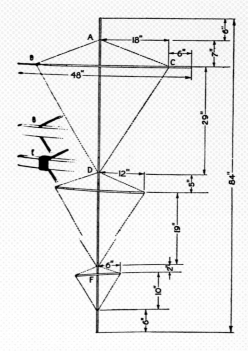

The spine with the bow sticks properly spaced as shown by the dimensions.

Nearly every boy can make kites of the several common varieties without special directions. For the boy who wants a kite that is not like those every other boy makes, an eight-pointed star kite, decorated in an original manner, is well worthwhile, even if it requires more careful work, and extra time. The star kite shown in *Figure 1* is simple in construction and, if carefully made, will fly to a great height. It is balanced by streamers instead of the common type of kite tail. Any regular-shaped kite should be laid out accurately, as otherwise the error appears very prominent and unbalances the poise of the kite.

The frame for this star kite is made of four sticks joined, as indicated in *Figure 5*, with strings running from one corner to the second corner beyond, as from *A* to *C*, from *C* to *E*, etc. A

Figure 1

little notching of each pair of sticks lessens the thickness of the sticks at the center crossing and strengthens the frame. The sticks are ¼ by ½ in. by 4 ft. long. They are set at right angles to each other in pairs and lashed together with cord. They are also held by a ¾-in. brad at the center. The strings that form the sides of the squares, A to G, and B to H, must be equal in length when tied. The points where the strings forming the squares cross each other and the sticks are also tied.

The first cover, which is put on with paste laying it out on a smooth floor or table as usual in kite making, is plain, light-colored paper. The darker decorations are pasted onto this. The outside edges of the cover are turned over the string outline and pasted down. The colors may be in many combinations, such as red and white, purple and gold, green and white, etc. Brilliant and contrasting colors are best. The decoration may proceed from the center out, or the reverse. The outside edge in the design shown has a 1 ½ in. black stripe. The figures

are black. The next octagonal black line binds the design together. The points of the star are dark blue with a gilt stripe on each. The center design is done in black, dark blue, and gilt.

The flags are tied on, and the tassels are easily made of cord. The outside streamers are at least 6 ft. long and balanced carefully. Ribbons or dark-colored lining cambric are used for them. The funnel-shaped ends balance the kite. They are shown in detail in *Figures 2*, *3*, and *4*, and have 1-inch openings at the bottom, through which the air passes, causing a pull that steadies the kite. They are of dark blue, and the cloth fringe is of light blue. A thin reed or fine wire is used for the hoop that stiffens the top. Heavy wrapping or cover paper is used to cover the hoop. It is cut as shown in *Figure 4* and rolled into shape.

A four-string bridle is fastened to the frame at *I*, *J*, *K*, and *L*, as shown. The upper strings are each 18 in., and the lower ones 32 in. long, to the point where they come together, and must be adjusted after the kite line is fastened at *M*.

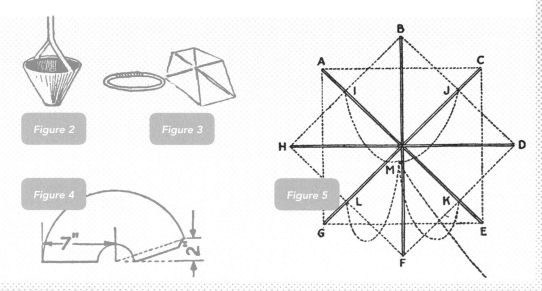

Figure 2

Figure 3

Figure 4

Figure 5

A serious kite-flying boy is not satisfied with simply holding the end of a kite string and running up and down the block or field trying to raise a heavy paper kite with a half-pound of rags for a tail. He makes a kite as light as possible without any tail, which has the peculiar property of being able to move in every direction. Sometimes an expert can make one of these kites travel across the wind for several hundred feet. In fact, I have seen boys a full block apart bring their kites together and engage in a combat until one of their kites floated away with a broken string, or was punctured by the swift dives of the other and sent to earth, a wreck.

The boy makes his kite as follows: From a sheet of thin but tough tissue paper about 20 in. square, which he folds and cuts along the dotted line as shown in *Figure 1*, he gets a perfectly square kite having all the properties of a good flyer, light and strong. He shapes two pieces of bamboo, one for the backbone and one for the bow. The backbone is flat, 1/4 by 3/32 in. and 18 in. long. This he smears along one side with common boiled rice. Boiled rice is one of the best adhesives for use on paper that can be obtained, and the Chinese have used it for centuries, while we are just waking up to the fact that it makes a fine photo paste. Having placed the backbone in position, paste two triangular pieces of paper over the ends of the stick to prevent tearing. The bow is now bent and the lugs extending from the sides of the square paper are bent over the ends of the bow and pasted down. If the rice is quite dry or mealy, it can be smeared on and will dry almost immediately; therefore no strings are needed to hold

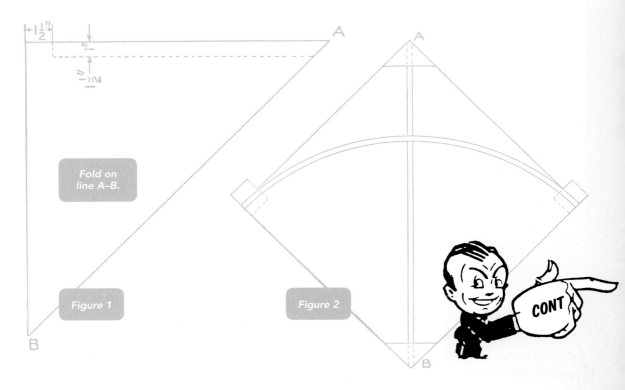

Fold on line A–B.

Figure 1

Figure 2

CONT

the bow bent while the paste dries.

After the sticks are in position, the kite will appear as shown in *Figure 2*. The dotted lines show the lugs bent over the ends of the bow and pasted down. *Figure 3* shows how the band is put on and how the kite is balanced. This is the most important part and cannot be explained very well. This must be done by experimenting, and it is enough to say that the kite must balance perfectly. The string is fastened by a slipknot to the band, moved back and forth until the kite flies properly, and then it is securely fastened.

A reel is made next. Two ends—the bottoms of two small peach baskets will do—are fastened to a dowel stick or broom handle, if nothing better is at hand. These ends are placed about 14 in. apart and strips nailed between them, as shown in *Figure 4*, and the center drawn in and bound with a string. The kite string used is generally a heavy packing thread. This is run through a thin flour or rice paste until it is thoroughly coated, then it is run through a quantity of crushed glass. The glass should be beaten up fine and run through a fine sieve to make it about the same as No. 2 emery. The particles should be extremely sharp and full of splinters. These particles adhere to the pasted string and when dry are so sharp that it cannot be handled without scratching the fingers. Therefore the kite is flown entirely from the reel. To wind the string upon the reel, all that is necessary is to lay one end of the reel stick in the

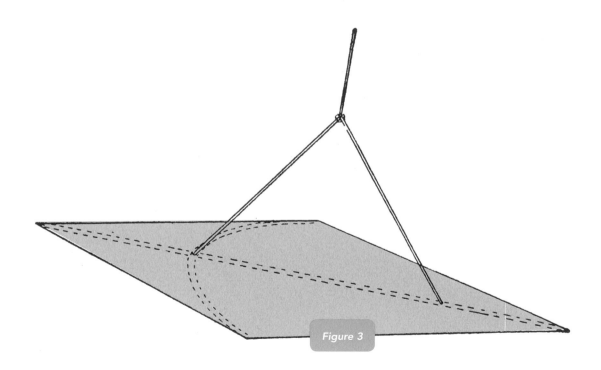

Figure 3

bend of the left arm and twirl the other end between the fingers of the right hand.

In China, a boy will be flying a gaily colored little kite from the roof of a house (if it is in one of the large cities that have flat-roofed houses) and a second boy will appear on the roof of another house perhaps 200 ft. away. Both have large reels full of string, often several hundred yards of it. The first hundred feet or so is glass-covered string, the balance common packing thread or glass-covered string. As soon as the second boy has his kite aloft, he begins maneuvering to drive it across the wind and over to the first kite. First, he pays out a large amount of string. Then, as the kite wobbles to one side with its nose pointing toward the first kite, he tightens his line and commences a steady quick pull. If properly done, his kite crosses over to the other and above it. The string is now paid out until the second kite is hanging over the first one's line. The wind now tends to take the second kite back to its parallel and in so doing makes a turn about the first kite's string. If the second kite is close enough, the first tries to spear him by swift dives. The second boy in the meantime is see-sawing his string and presently the first kite's string is cut and it drifts away.

It is not considered sport to haul the other fellow's kite down as might be done, and therefore a very interesting battle is often witnessed when the experts clash their kites.

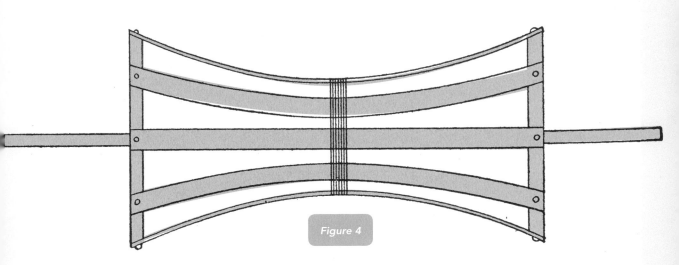

Figure 4

How To MAKE A WAR KITE

The material required is three pine sticks, each 60 in. long, one stick 54 in. long, one stick 18 in. long, all ½ in. square; 4 yards of cambric; a box of tacks; some linen thread; and 16 ft. of stout twine.

Place two 60-in. sticks parallel with each other and 18 in. apart. Then lay the 54-in. piece across at right angles to them 18 in. from the upper ends, as shown in *Figure 1*, and fasten the joints with brads. At a point 21 in. below this crosspiece, attach the 18-in. crosspiece.

The extending ends of all three long pieces are notched, *Figure 2*, and the line is stretched taut around them as shown by the dotted lines. If the cambric is not of sufficient size to cover the frame, two pieces must be sewn together. Then a piece is cut out to the shape of the string, allowing 1 in. to project all around for a lap. The cambric is sewn

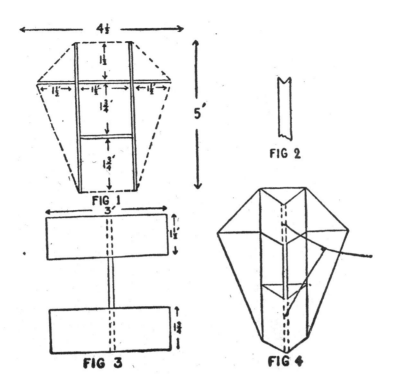

FIG 1

FIG 2

FIG 3

FIG 4

fast to the string with the linen thread. Fasten the cloth to the frame part with the tacks, spacing them 1 in. apart. The space in the center, between the sticks, is cut out. Make two pieces of the remaining goods, one 36 in. by 18 in. and the other 36 in. by 21 in. The remaining 60-in. stick is fastened to these pieces of cambric, as shown in *Figure 3*, and the whole is fastened to the main frame so as to make a V-shaped projection. The bridle strings, for giving the proper distribution of pull on the line to the kite, are fastened one to the upper end of the long stick in the V-shaped piece attached to the kite. The other is fastened to the lower end, as shown in *Figure 4*. The inclination can be varied to suit the builder by changing the point of attachment of the kite line to the bridle. If it is desired to fly the kite directly overhead, attach the line above the regular point. For low flying, make the connection below this point. The regular point is found by trial flights with the line fastened temporarily to the bridle, after which the fastening is made permanent.

The kite being tailless rides the airwaves like an aeroplane in a steady breeze.

After building a number of kites from recent description in *Amateur Mechanics*, I branched out and constructed the aeroplane kite shown in the illustration, which has excited considerable comment in the neighborhood on account of its appearance and behavior in the air.

The main frame consists of a 31-in.-long center stick, *A*, and two cross sticks, of which one, *B*, is 31 in. long and the other, *C*, 15 ½ in. long. The location of the crosspieces on the centerpiece *A* is shown in the sketch, the front piece *B* being 1 ¾ in. from the end, and the rear piece *C*, 2 ¼ in. from the other end. The ends of the sticks have small notches cut to receive a string, *D*, which is run around the outside to make the outline of the frame and to brace the parts. Two cross strings are placed at *E* and *F*, 7 in. from either end of the centerpiece *A*. Other brace strings are crossed, as shown in *G*, and then tied to the cross string *F* on both sides, as in *H*.

The long crosspiece *B* is curved upward to form a bow, the center of which should be 3 ¼ in. above the string by which its ends are tied together. The shorter crosspiece is bent and tied in the same manner to make the curve 2 ½ in., and the centerpiece to curve 1 ¾ in., both upward. The front and rear parts, between the end and the cross strings *E* and *F*, are covered with yellow tissue paper. This is pasted to the crosspieces and strings. The small wings *L* are purple tissue paper, 4 in. wide at *M* and tapering to a point at *N*.

The bridle string is attached on the centerpiece *A*, at the junction of the crosspieces *B* and *C*, and must be adjusted for the size and weight of the kite. The kite is tailless and requires a steady breeze to make it float in the air currents like an aeroplane.

The bridle string and the bending of the sticks must be adjusted until the desired results are obtained. The bridle string should be tied so that it will about center under the cross stick *B* for the best results. But a slight change from this location may be necessary to make the kite ride the air currents properly. The center of gravity will not be the same in the construction of each kite, and the string can be located only by trial, after which it is permanently fastened.

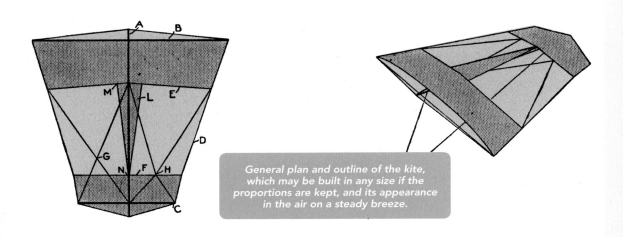

General plan and outline of the kite, which may be built in any size if the proportions are kept, and its appearance in the air on a steady breeze.

This kite reel is constructed from two old pulleys and a few pipe fittings. The large pulley is about 14 in. in diameter, on the face of which are riveted flat strips of iron with extending arms. These arms are reinforced by riveting smaller pieces from one to the other. If you like high-flying kites, this is an efficient way to handle your kite line.

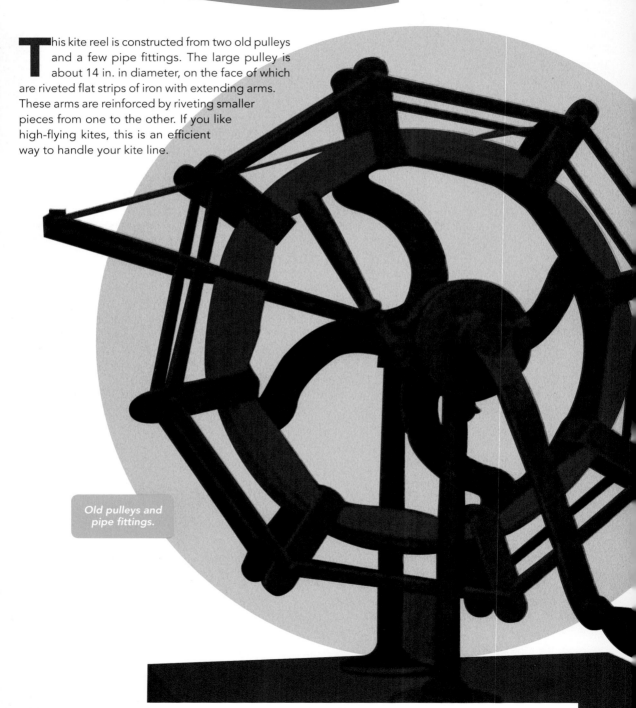

Old pulleys and pipe fittings.

Parachutes carried up to a lofty kite, and automatically released when the carrier hits a cross stick tied in the kite line, will keep up a lively interest. The carrier must be lightweight and there should be very little friction on the line so that ascent of the carrier will not be impeded. A cardboard sail and a parachute are held on a sliding member, which is pushed back when it strikes the cross stick, releasing sail and parachute. By going over the details, you will see how the device works.

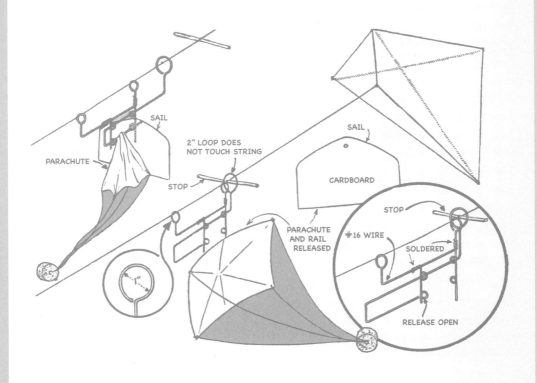

CAMERA FOR TAKING PICTURES FROM A KITE

When watching a kite flying at a considerable height, one frequently wonders how the landscape appears from such a viewpoint as would be possible from a kite. Few of us can have the experience of a ride in an airplane, but it is quite possible to obtain a view from the kite, by proxy as it were, through the use of a kite camera. A kite of large dimensions would be necessary to carry an ordinary camera taking pictures of fair size; hence it is necessary to devise a camera of lighter construction so that a kite of moderate size may carry it to a height of several hundred feet. Such a camera is shown in the illustration, attached to a box kite. Details of construction are shown in the smaller sketches.

A camera consists, briefly, of a lightproof box with a lens at one end and a sensitive plate of film at the other. For a kite camera, a single achromatic lens will suit the purpose. Such a lens is not expensive and may be taken from a small camera. It must be obtained before the camera is begun, because the size of the camera is dependent upon the focal length of the lens and the size of the picture to be made. A camera taking pictures 2 in. square is satisfactory for kite photography. If it is desired to enlarge the pictures, this may be done in the usual manner.

The box of the camera is made cone-shaped in order to reduce the weight and air resistance. Its sides are of lightweight, stiff cardboard, reinforced at the corners to ensure that no light will enter. The back of the camera is a tight-fitting cover of cardboard having the same measurements as the picture to be taken. The lens is fitted to an intermediate partition, as shown in the sketch. It is necessary to determine the focal length of the lens and to set it at a distance from the inner side of the cardboard back of the camera— the film surface—so that it will focus properly for photographing distant objects.

The front is provided with a circular opening of a size large enough not to obstruct the view of the lens. A shutter made of thin pressboard is fitted over the opening, as shown in the sketch on page 38. A slit is cut in the shutter through which light is admitted in making the exposure as the shutter

CAMERA

The kite camera offers a diversion in photography and has practical and commercial uses. The camera shown is of lightweight, simple construction, and produces film exposures 2 in. square.

CONT

is drawn back. The size and width of the slit regulates the exposure, and a few trials must be made to determine the most suitable speed of exposure for the lens used. The shutter is pivoted at its lower end and drawn back by a rubber band. A string, to which a time fuse is attached, controls the releasing of the shutter to make the exposure. The string holds the shutter closed against the pull of the rubber band until the fuse burns up to the string, severing it. The fuse must be long enough to enable the kite to attain a suitable height before the string is burned. When the shutter has been set and the fuse attached ready for lighting, the camera may be taken into the darkroom for loading. A piece of film, cut to the proper size, is placed carefully into the light-proof sliding cover, as with a film pack. The sensitive side is, of course, placed nearest the lens.

The camera is attached to the kite securely at the middle, as shown, so that when the kite is in flight, a view nearly straight down will be obtained. When all is in readiness, the fuse is lighted and the kite started on its flight. By timing experimental flights, the required length of fuse may be determined in order to permit the kite to attain the desired height at the time of exposure.

The kite used for taking pictures from the air should be large enough to carry the camera easily. One of the box type illustrated is satisfactory, although other types may be used. A kite camera for the amateur has great possibilities for experimentation, but requires care in construction and a reasonable knowledge of photography. To the person willing to master the details, kite photography offers a pleasurable diversion as well as practical uses in photographing plots of ground, groups of buildings, manufacturing plants, and other subjects that cannot be photographed by other methods.

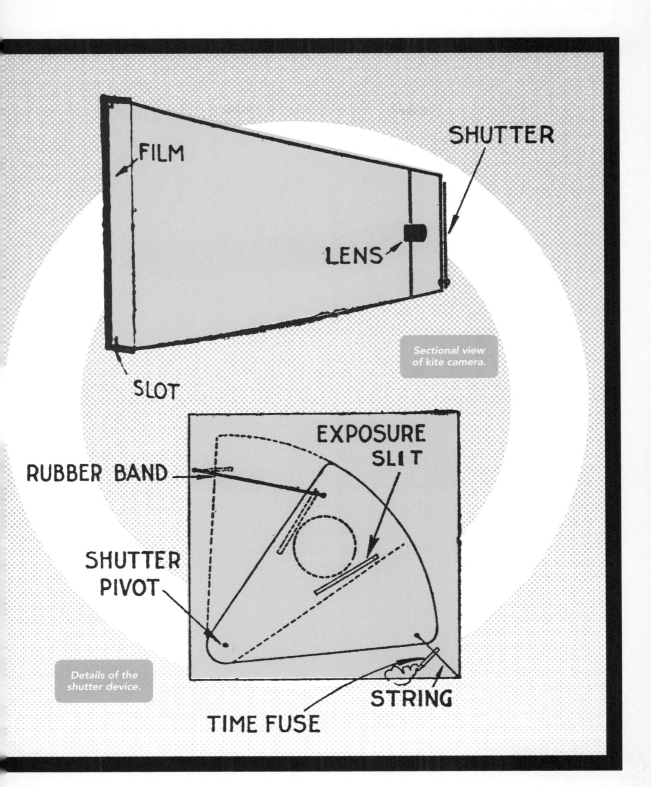

FILM

SHUTTER

LENS

SLOT

Sectional view of kite camera.

RUBBER BAND

EXPOSURE SLIT

SHUTTER PIVOT

STRING

Details of the shutter device.

TIME FUSE

PAPER GLIDER THAT LOOPS THE LOOP

The usual paper glider shaped as shown in *Figure 1* can be made to loop the loop and make corkscrew flights if prepared according to sketches herewith. It should be carefully made in the first place so that in its regular form it flies perfectly straight.

To make the glider loop, the rear corners of the wings should be turned up at right angles, as in *Figure 2*, and the glider launched with a great deal of force with the nose pointed slightly upward. This will require some practice, but one soon learns the trick. After looping once, as shown in *Figure 3*, the glider descends in volplane. This form of glider will also right itself if dropped from a height, nose downward, as shown in *Figure 4*.

For a corkscrew flight, the glider is prepared as in *Figure 5*; one rear corner being bent up and the other down. In this form, it flies horizontally, or downward, while rapidly rotating around its longitudinal axis, as shown in *Figure 6*.

To make a spiral descent, the rear corners of the wings are bent up as in *Figure 2*, and the rear corner of the keel is bent at right angles, *Figure 7*, whereupon it is thrown in the ordinary manner. It then takes the course shown in *Figure 8*.

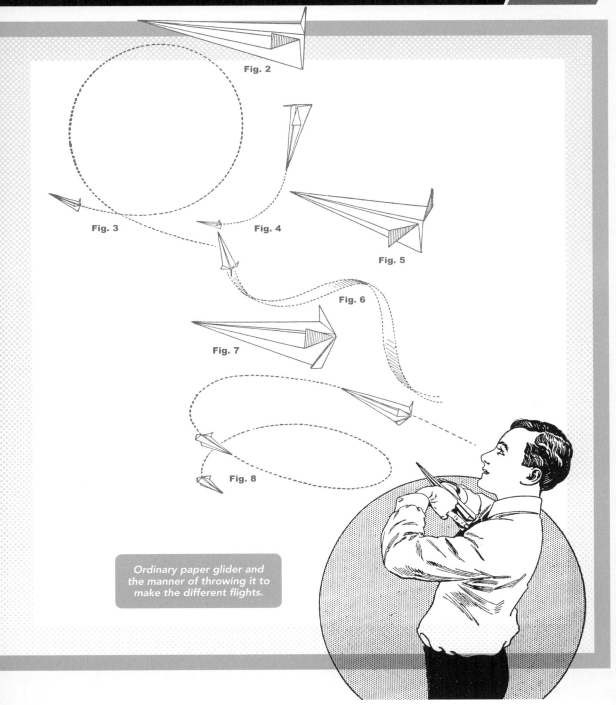

Fig. 1

Fig. 2

Fig. 3

Fig. 4

Fig. 5

Fig. 6

Fig. 7

Fig. 8

Ordinary paper glider and the manner of throwing it to make the different flights.

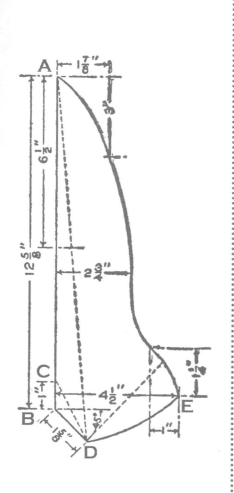

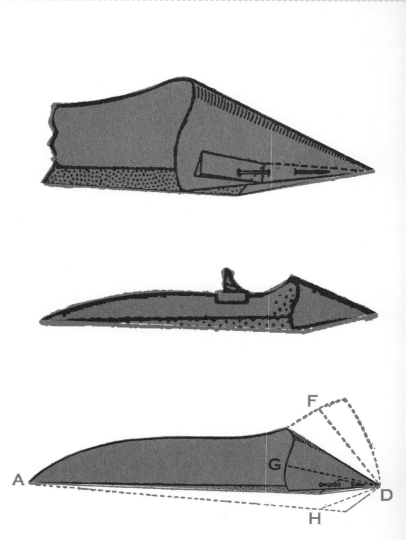

TOY PAPER GLIDER CAREFULLY DESIGNED

A paper glider is an interesting and useful toy that can be made quickly. It may be used out of doors, but occasions when weather conditions make it necessary to remain indoors are especially good for this form of pastime. The glider shown in the sketch was worked out after considerable testing. With a toss, it travels 20 to 30 ft. on a level keel, with a message slipped behind a pin, as shown in the upper sketch. The inventive boy may devise many play uses for the glider, in tournaments, competitions, and for "military" flights, in which the "drivers" of the devices may "annihilate armies." Practical use of the toy was made in a series of air-current tests.

The glider is made as follows: Fold a piece of 10- by 15-in. paper lengthwise, and mark the outline shown at the left upon it. The dimensions should be followed carefully. Measure first from the end *A* to the point *B*, and then draw the slanting line to *D*, at an angle of 45 degrees. Mark the width to *E*, and measure the other distances from *A* and at the middle, to determine the curve of the edge. Mark the dotted lines extending from *D*, which are guides for the folding of the paper to form the glider, as shown in the lower sketch. Curl the points under the side so that the line *FD* comes to the position *DG*, and pin them to the corners *H*, as shown in the lower sketch. The glider is tossed by holding it between the thumb and forefinger at the middle of the fold underneath it.

An interesting bit of paper construction is a small monoplane made from a 7-in. square of paper, folded as indicated in the diagram, and provided with a paper tail. This little monoplane can be steered by adjusting the tail and can even be made to loop the loop in varying air currents.

To make this model, fold a square of medium-weight paper on the dotted lines as indicated in *Figure 1*. Then unfold the sheet and refold it as in *Figure 2*. Then bring the folded corners *A* and *B* into position as shown in *A* and *B* in *Figure 3*. Fold the corners *C* and *D* upward to the position *C* and *D* in *Figure 4*. Fold corners

G and *H* to the corresponding letters in *Figure 5*. Fold points *J* and *K* to the corresponding letters in *Figure 6*. Raise the points *J* and *K*, *Figure 6*, and fold them in so that the corners that were below them in *Figure 6* now come above them, as in *L* and *M* in *Figure 7*. Fold the corner *N* back along the line *OP*, *Figure 8*, so that the shape

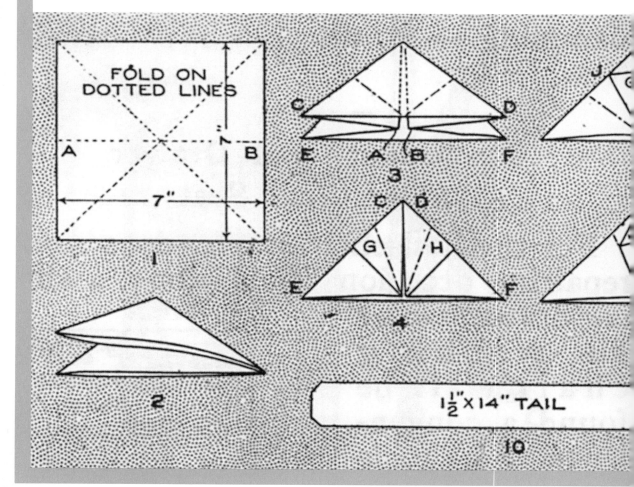

FOLD ON DOTTED LINES

7"

1½"X14" TAIL

of the main portion of the model is as shown in *Figure 9*, in *OP*. Make the tail 1 ½ by 14 in. long, as shown in *Figure 10*, and paste it into position. This completes the model, which can be steered by bending or twisting the tail.

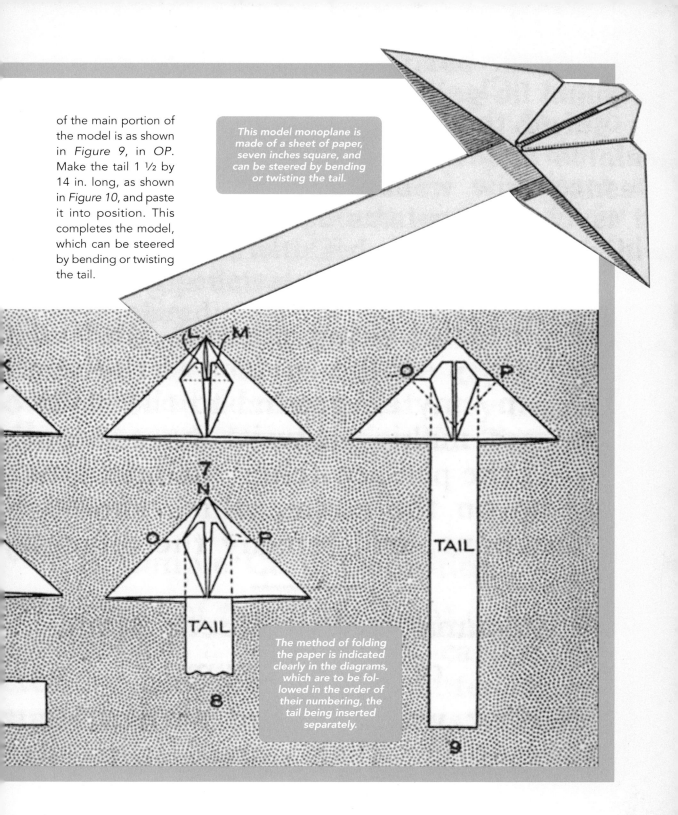

This model monoplane is made of a sheet of paper, seven inches square, and can be steered by bending or twisting the tail.

The method of folding the paper is indicated clearly in the diagrams, which are to be followed in the order of their numbering, the tail being inserted separately.

BUILD MODEL AIRPLANES

The model airplanes illustrated, while they do not exemplify the very best performance or design, nevertheless have proved to be very satisfactory in flight. They also include structural features that make them easy to build. Because of this simplicity of design, they will appeal to the person who likes to build, whether he has the experience in this line or not. He will be able to complete the style of his choice, provided he has the necessary patience and consideration for detail.

Because the "racer," *Figure 1,* the "fly-about," *Figure 2,* and the "rise-off-ground," *Figure 9,* are nearly alike, they will be described first. The wings of all three are built up in the same manner, using materials of the same kind, but differing in their dimensions. To build the wings for any of these, two strips of white pine, basswood, or spruce are selected. They should be a trifle over the required length, and planed down to measure

exactly 1/8 by 1/4 in., and then cut to length. Mark the middle of the strips and drill a 1/16-in. hole through each. In the center of each end of the strips, drill a 1/16-in. hole 1/2 in. deep. Next, cut several strips of tough paper

One of the model planes in flight.

1 in. wide, coat them with glue, and bind each end and the middle of the spars, wrapping two or three thicknesses of paper around them. This is to prevent splitting. From a piece of soft wire, 1/16 in. in diameter, cut a piece 1 in. longer than the distance between the centers of the spars and bend right angles

1/2 in. from each end. Flatten the ends of the wires on an anvil or vise, lay the spars flat on a smooth surface, and insert the short ends of the wires into the holes in the ends of the strips. Force them in as far as they will go, as indicated in *Figure 5.* When these wires are bent to control the direction of flight, they will stay so, because they are soft and because the flattened ends prevent them from moving up and down. This method bends the rear spar a little, but it has proved satisfactory on many models. After the wing frame has been assembled, lay it on a piece of tough paper, mark the outline, and then cut it out, leaving a 1/2-in. margin on all sides. Now coat the underside of the frame with glue and place it on the paper, with the margin even all around. Work out the wrinkles, being careful not to bow in the spars. Cut the ends of the paper to fit between the spars, coat them with glue, fold over the wires, and stick to the top

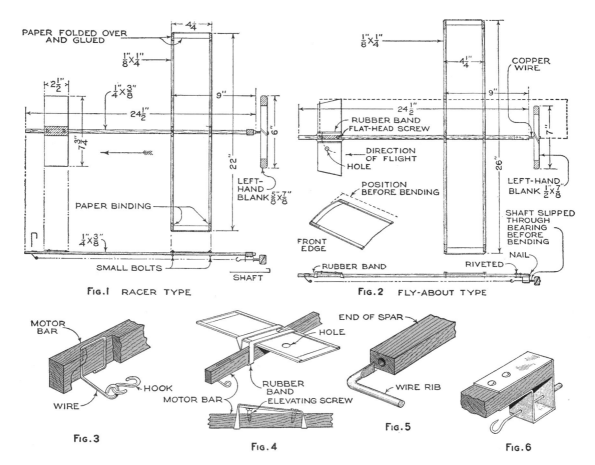

FIG. 1 RACER TYPE

FIG. 2 FLY-ABOUT TYPE

FIG. 3

FIG. 4

FIG. 5

FIG. 6

side of the paper. After the glue has dried thoroughly, lay the wing on a smooth board and trim off the surplus paper. Punch a hole through the paper binding over the holes in the spars, and give the whole a coat of waterproof varnish to make an exceedingly tough and durable unit.

For the motor bar, cut a piece of pine or spruce, ¼ by ⅜ by 24 ½ in. Lay it flat, drill a 1/16-in. hole about ¾ in. from one end, and another ½ in. from the first. Bend a piece of soft wire as in *Figure 3*, slip it through the holes, and bend the ends as shown. The propeller bearing on the racer is made from a piece of sheet metal, drilled for the 1/16-in. diameter shaft, and fastened to the bar as shown in *Figure 6*. It can be bound to the shaft with glued paper, which will, perhaps, be the better way for the beginner.

Figure 7 shows how to make the propeller. The shaft should be made of wire, bent as shown in *Figure 1*, and slipped through the hole drilled in the center of the propeller. By indenting the hub a little with the short end of the shaft, the exact position for the extra hole can be found. When this is drilled, slip the shaft through the hub again, pressing the short

end into the extra hole. This prevents any chance of the propeller turning on its shaft. Another way is to flatten the end of the shaft and force the widened part into the wood, parallel with the grain.

The elevator, *Figure 4*, is made of pine or basswood. It is bound in the middle with glued paper, as described for the wing spars and indicated by the shaded section in

Figure 1. Plane down the wood to 1/16 in. in thickness, and cut a piece of the proper size; for the racer, it should measure 2 1/2 by 8 in., for the fly-about 2 1/2 by 8 1/2 in., and for the rise-off-ground model 3 by 9 in. Bind the edges with a strip of paper and varnish. The elevator of the racer is not movable but is attached with two round-head screws to the motor bar. This

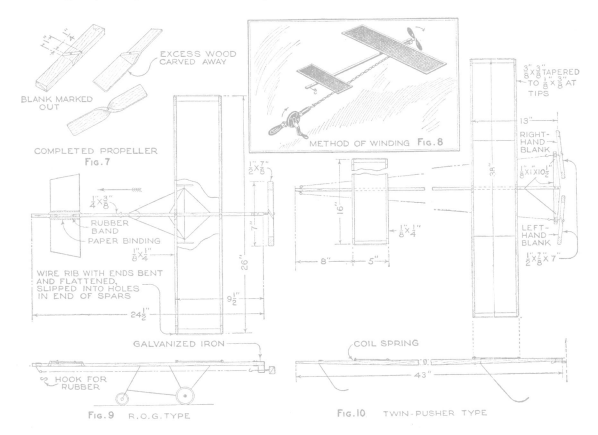

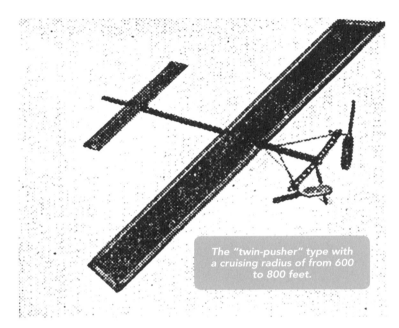

The "twin-pusher" type with a cruising radius of from 600 to 800 feet.

makes it impossible to alter the angle of the elevator on this model without removing it from the bar. Two or three small washers underneath the forward edge serve to place it at the correct angle. On the fly-about and rise-off-ground models, however, the elevator is adjustable, and is fastened with but one screw near the rear edge. This serves as a pivot. Use a rubber band to hold the elevator down against a flat-headed screw located under the front edge, and keep it straight. To increase or decrease the angle of the elevator, merely turn it to one side, so that

the hole shown in the drawing will come over the screw head. Then, with a small screwdriver, turn the screw in or out as needed, and allow the elevator to return to its normal position. The rubber band also prevents the elevator from breaking by absorbing some of the landing shock.

The rise-off-ground model, *Figure 9*, is just like the fly-about, except that it has a little more surface than the latter, and the wing is set at an angle large enough to give it a good lift. This is done with small washers or coiled wire of sufficient thickness to raise the front

wing spar about ⅛ in. The drawing shows how the landing gear, which consists of three wheels mounted on hard wire, is attached. Make the wheels of cigar-box wood, drill the centers, and use the same size of wire for the axles as for the wire supports. The ends should be looped around the axles. The small front wheel must be a little lower than the others so that the forward end of the motor bar will be higher than the rear when the model is resting on the ground. The diameter of the front wheel is 1 ½ in., and the larger ones are 2 in. in diameter.

The "twin pusher," *Figure 10*, is more elaborate than the other three but is not beyond the amateur's ability. Its elevator does not swing, but it is made in exactly the same manner as the other models. This is also true of the wing, except that in this case the spars are ⅜ in. square in the middle, tapered down to ⅛ by ⅜ in. at their tips. Two extra wire ribs are placed 6 in. from the center between the spars. The holes are drilled and the ribs inserted before the paper wing covering is applied. The motor bar is of pine or spruce, ½ by 1

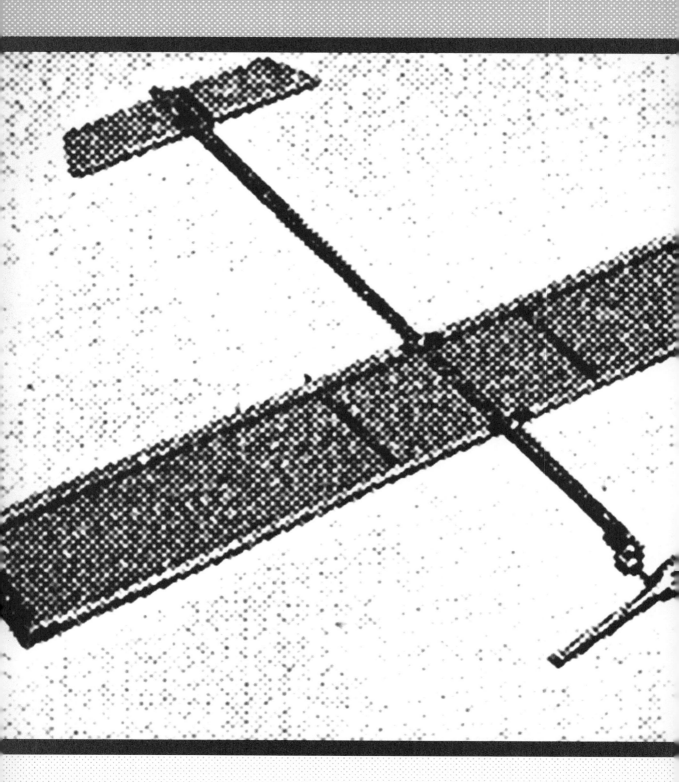

by 43 in., shaped as shown in the drawing. Make the front hook from a 4-in. length of wire, insert it in a small hole drilled near the front of the bar, and bend the loops. The crossbar that takes the bearings should be of ash or other hardwood, and be braced with $\frac{1}{16}$-in. hard wire. The bearings are strips of sheet metal, bent to U-shape and riveted to the crossbar. Hard wire is used for the landing skids. The front edge of the wing should be raised about $\frac{1}{16}$ in. The elevator is adjustable and is attached to the motor bar by two screws. The front one runs through a small coil spring between the spar and motor bar, and furnishes a means of changing the angle of the elevator.

The power on all these models is furnished by rubber bands, about $\frac{3}{64}$ in. thick, $\frac{3}{16}$ in. wide, and 4 in. long. They should be linked together chain fashion, so that three of the bands will only make a length of 6 in. instead of 12 in. This method allows broken bands to be replaced with new ones quickly and easily.

A wire hook, inserted in the chuck of a hand drill, as shown in *Figure 8*, will serve as a winder. After linking the bands together on the mold, release the front end of the "motor,"

and hook it to the drill. Stretch the rubber to about twice its length and turn until about half wound. Then keep turning, but gradually release the tension so that the rubber will be straight when fully wound, and hook on again. The number of turns needed will be found through experience; the twin model will stand more than 1,000 turns to each propeller, which means that with a gear ratio of 4 to 1 on the drill, the handle will have to be turned 250 times. The two propellers on this model must revolve in opposite directions.

To launch, hold the motor bar with the right hand, just ahead of the wing, and the propeller with the left. Then, with a quick upward push, send the airplane into the air. If it has a tendency to climb too steeply, the elevator should be lowered a little; if it loses altitude, the elevator should be raised enough to correct this fault. With both wingtips flat, the planes will have a tendency to turn to the right. Curving the right wingtip down a little will give a straightaway flight; a left turn can be made by curving the right tip down still more. Several trial flights will probably be necessary before the proper adjustment is obtained.

MAKE A MODEL OLD-FOUR MONOPLANE

The old-four monoplane model, made famous by its wonderful flights, is one of the most graceful that has been built. Its large size and slow, even glide make it a much more desirable flier than the ordinary dart-like model. It gives one a true insight into the phenomena of heavier-than-air flight. This machine, when complete, should weigh 9 oz. and fly 1,200 ft., rising from the ground under its own power and landing lightly. Its construction is simple, and with careful reference to the sketches, an exact reproduction may be made.

For the motor bases, A, *Figure 1*, secure two spruce sticks, each 48 in. long, 3/8 in. wide, and 1/4 in. thick. Fasten a wire hook on one end of each stick with thread wound around after giving it a coat of glue. These hooks are to hold one end of the rubber bands that act as the motive power, and are designated by the letter B. At the opposite ends of the sticks, at C, bearings are provided. These consist of blocks of wood, each 1 in. long, 1 in. wide, and 3/8 in. thick. These are also bound in place with thread after gluing them. Holes are drilled through the blocks lengthwise and then lined with bushings made of brass tubing, 1/16 in. in inside diameter. The two motor bases A are connected with four cross sticks, D, each 9 in. long and 3/16 in. square. These are bound and glued on the underside, one near each end and the others equidistant each from the other and from the nearest end stick. The front bumper, E, is made of round rattan, 1/8 in. in diameter.

The mechanical bird will run about five feet on the ground and then rise and fly.

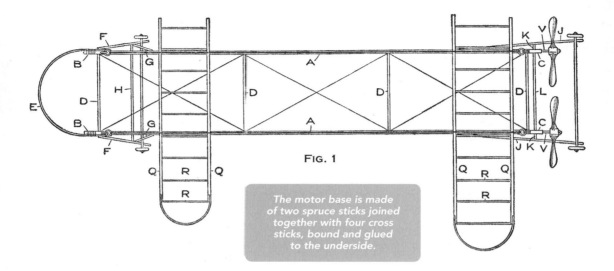

FIG. 1

The motor base is made of two spruce sticks joined together with four cross sticks, bound and glued to the underside.

The alighting gear is next in order of construction. This is made, as shown, entirely of bamboo 3/16 in. square. The pieces marked F are 11 in. long; G, 9 1/2 in. long; and the crossbar H, 11 in. long. At the rear, the pieces J are 13 in. long; K, 4 1/2 in. long; and the crosspiece L, 11 in. long. The distance between the points M and N, Figure 2, is 6 in., and between O and P, 9 in. The bamboo is easily curved by wetting and holding it for an instant in the flame of a candle. It will hold its shape just as soon as it becomes cold. The wheels are made of tin, 1 1/2 in. in diameter, borrowed from a toy automobile. The axles are made from wire, 1/16 in. in diameter.

The wing spars Q are made of spruce, 3/16 in. wide and 1/4 in. thick. Those for the front are 30 in. long, and for the rear, 36 in. long. The ribs R are made of bamboo pieces, 1/16 in. square, 5 in. long for the front plane, and 6 in. for the rear. These are bound and glued on top of the spars, 3 in. apart. They are given a slight upward curve. The round ends are made of 1/16-in. rattan.

It is rather difficult to make good propellers, but with a little time and patience they can be shaped and formed into good proportions. Procure two clear, straight-grained blocks of white pine, 8 in. long, 1 1/2 in. wide, and 3/4 in. thick. Draw a diagonal line on one block from opposite corners as shown in S, Figure 3,

then on the other block T, draw the line in an opposite direction. Turn the blocks over and draw opposite diagonals, as shown by the dotted lines. Draw a circle on each side exactly on the center, 1/2 in. in diameter. Drill 1/16-in. holes through the centers of the circles for the propeller shafts. The wood is then cut down to the lines drawn, leaving only enough materials that they will not break easily. The face of the blades should be flat and the back rounded. Leave plenty of stock near the hub. After the faces have been finished, the blades are shaped as shown at U. The propellers should be finished with sandpaper to make them perfectly smooth, as much of the success of the model will depend upon them. It is wise to shellac them and also the frame and the alighting gear. Aluminum paint costs but little, and it makes a fine finish for a model aeroplane.

The propeller shafts, *V*, *Figures 1*, *2*, and *4*, are cut from bicycle spokes. An eye for the rubber band is bent in the spoke, about 2 in. from the threaded end. The end having the threads is run through the bearing block, *C*, *Figure 4*, and the propeller fastened on with a small washer on each side of it by means of two nuts, *W*, cut from a bicycle nipple. These nuts may be turned up tightly with pliers.

The planes are covered with tissue paper put on tightly over the tops of the ribs, using a flour paste. The planes are movably fixed on the motor bases *A* by tying at the four points of contact with rubber bands. This makes it possible to adjust the fore-and-aft balance of the machine by changing the position of the planes.

The motive power, which is the most important part of the entire machine, consists of rubber bands. There are three ways of obtaining these bands. It is best, if possible, to purchase them from an aeroplane supply house. In this case, procure about 100 ft. of 1/16-in. square rubber, 50 ft. for each side. These are wound closely between the hooks *X*. This rubber can be taken from a golf ball. It will require about 40 strands of this rubber on each propeller. The rubber is removed by cutting into the ball. Another way of obtaining the bands is to purchase No. 19 rubber bands and loop them together, chain-fashion, to make them long enough to reach between the hooks without stretching. About 30 strands on each propeller will be sufficient. The hooks *X* are made in the shape of the letter "S," to provide a way for taking out the rubber bands quickly. To prevent the hooks from cutting the rubber, slip some 1/16-in. rubber tubing over them. The rubber bands, or motor, when not

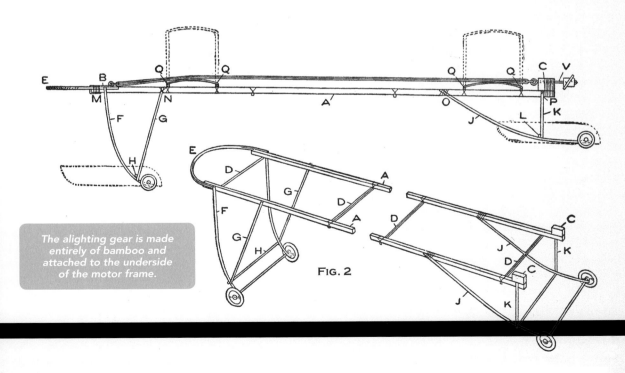

The alighting gear is made entirely of bamboo and attached to the underside of the motor frame.

FIG. 2

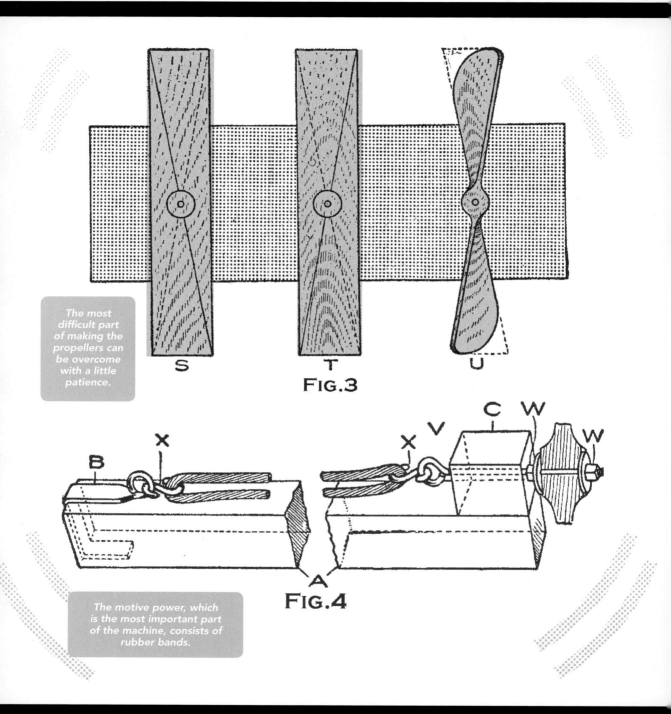

The most difficult part of making the propellers can be overcome with a little patience.

S T U

FIG.3

The motive power, which is the most important part of the machine, consists of rubber bands.

FIG.4

in use, should be kept in a cool, dark place and powdered with French chalk to prevent the parts from sticking together.

With the model complete, flying is the next thing in order. With a machine as large as this one, quite a field will be necessary to give it a good flight. Test the plane by gliding it, that is, holding it up by the propellers and bearing blocks on a level with your head and throwing it forward on an even keel. Shift the planes forward or back until it balances and comes to the ground lightly.

Winding up the propellers is accomplished by means of an eye inserted in the chuck of an ordinary hand drill. While an assistant grasps the propellers and motor bearings, the rubber is unhooked from the front of the machine and hooked into the eye in the drill. Stretch the rubber out for about 10 ft., and as it is wound up, let it draw back gradually. Wind up the propellers in opposite directions, turning them from 4,000 to 800 revolutions. Be sure to wind both propellers the same number of turns, as this will assure a straight flight.

Set the machine on the ground and release both propellers at once, and at the same time push it forward. If everything is properly constructed and well balanced, the mechanical bird will run about 5 ft. on the ground and then rise to 15 or 20 ft. and fly from 800 to 1,200 ft., descending in a long glide and alighting gracefully.

If the machine fails to rise, move the forward plane toward the front. If it climbs up suddenly and hangs in the air and falls back on its tail, move it toward the back.

After the novelty of overland flights has worn off, try flights over the water. To do this, the wheels must be removed and four pontoons put in their place, as shown by the dotted lines in *Figure 2*.

Patience is the one thing necessary in model building. Sometimes a machine carefully made will not fly, and no one can make it do so until some seemingly unimportant alteration is made.

Framework for constructing pontoons by covering them with writing paper soaked in paraffin.

FIG.5

THROW TOYS

A FEATHER AIRPLANE DART

Four feathers, a nail, and some string are all the materials needed for making a glider that will fly gracefully through the air for considerable distances.

The feathers are cut and fitted together as shown in the drawing, the nail being placed horizontally in front of the wings, to keep the glider "trimmed."

The feather dart is shot in the same manner as a paper dart, and because the feathers are stronger, it will last much longer than a paper version.

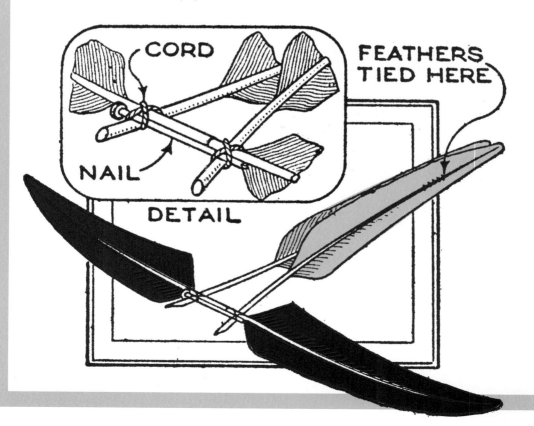

CORD

FEATHERS TIED HERE

NAIL

DETAIL

A SIMPLE AERIAL TOY

An interesting little toy that involves no more than a small piece of tin and an empty thread spool can be made in a few minutes. Two small wire brads are driven into one end of the spool, at diametrically opposite points. The heads are clipped off, leaving studs, ¾ in. long. A "whirler" is made from a piece of tin in the form of an airplane propeller, the blades being bent in opposite directions, as indicated. Holes to permit the propeller to make an easy fit on the studs are provided at the proper points. In use, the spool is placed on a shouldered stick, slightly smaller than the hole of the spool. Then about 4 ft. of strong twine is wrapped around the spool and the propeller is placed on the studs. Holding the spool by its shaft in one hand, the string is given a sharp pull with the other hand, and the propeller flies off into space.

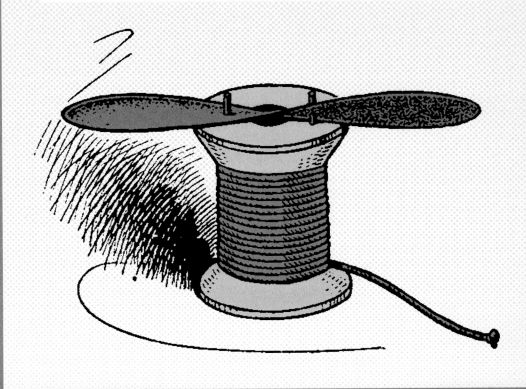

A boomerang is a weapon invented and used by native Australians. The boomerang is a curved stick of hardwood, *Figure 1*, about 5/16 in. thick by 2 1/2 in. wide by 2 ft. long, flat on one side with the ends and the other side rounding. One end of the stick is grasped in one hand with the convex edge forward and the flat side up, and thrown upward. After going some distance and ascending slowly to a great height in the air with a quick rotary motion, it suddenly returns in an elliptical orbit to a spot near the starting point. If thrown down on the ground, the boomerang rebounds in a straight line, pursuing a ricochet motion until the object is struck at which it was thrown.

Two other types of boomerangs are illustrated herewith and they can be made as described. The materials necessary for the T-shaped boomerang are: one piece of hard maple 5/16 in. thick by 2 1/2 in. wide by 3 ft. long; five 1/2 in. flathead screws. Cut the piece of hard maple into two pieces, one 11 1/2 in. and the other 18 in. long. The corners are cut from these pieces, as shown in *Figure 2*, taking care to cut exactly the same amount from each corner. Bevel both sides of the pieces, making the edges very thin so they will cut the air better. Find the exact center of the long piece and make a line 1 1/4 in. on each side of the center, and fasten the short length between the lines with the screws, as shown in *Figure 3*. The short piece should be fastened perfectly square and at right angles to the long one.

The materials necessary for the cross-shaped boomerang are one piece hard maple 5/16 in. thick by 2 in. wide by 30 in. long, and five 1/2-in. flathead screws. Cut the maple into two 14-in. pieces and plane the edges of these pieces so that the ends will be 1 1/2 in. wide, as shown in *Figure 4*. Bevel these pieces the same as the ones for the T-shaped boomerang. The two pieces are fastened together as shown in *Figure 5*. All of the boomerangs when completed should be given several coats of linseed oil and thoroughly dried. This will keep the wood from absorbing water and becoming heavy. The last two boomerangs are thrown in a similar way to the first one, except that one of the pieces is grasped in the hand and the throw given with a quick underhand motion. A little practice is all that is necessary for one to become skillful in throwing them.

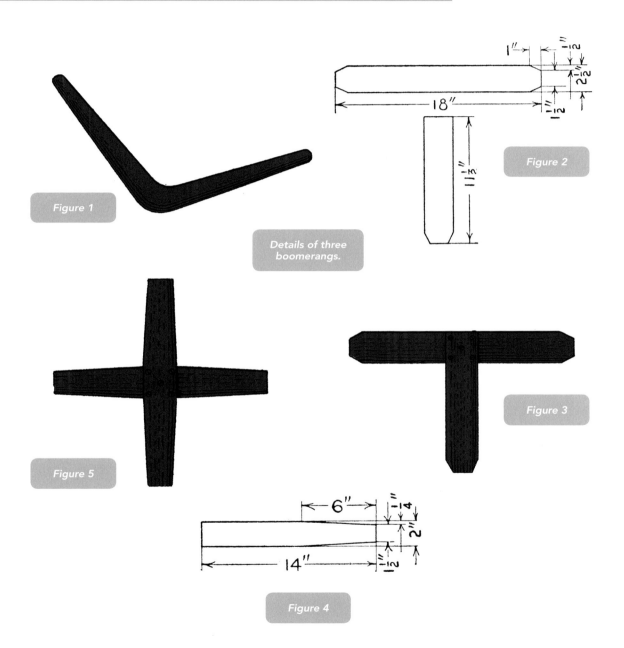

Figure 1

Figure 2

18"

1"

1"
1½

2½"

1½"

11½"

Details of three
boomerangs.

Figure 5

Figure 3

Figure 4

6"

14"

1¼"

2"

1½"

MORE BOOMERANGS

When the ice is too thin for skating and the snow is not right for skis, about the only thing to do is to stay in the house. A boomerang club will help to fill these in-between times, and also furnishes good exercise for the muscles of the arm. A boomerang can be made of a piece of well-seasoned hickory plank. The plank is steamed in a wash boiler or other large kettle and then bent to a nice curve, as shown in *Figure 1*. It is held in this curve until dry, with two pieces nailed on the sides, as shown. After the piece is thoroughly dried out, remove the sidepieces and cut into sections with a saw, as shown in *Figure 2*. The pieces are then dressed round. A piece of plank 12 in. wide and 2 ft. long will make six boomerangs.

To throw a boomerang, grasp and hold it the same as a club, with the hollow side away from you. Practice first at some object about 25 ft. distant, and in a short time you will be able to hit the mark over 100 ft. away. Any worker in wood can turn out a great number of boomerangs cheaply.

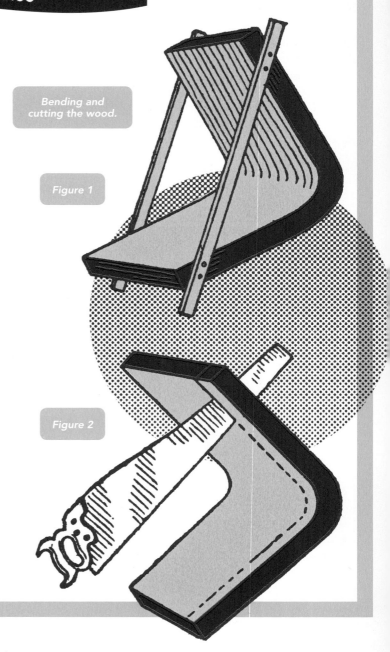

Bending and cutting the wood.

Figure 1

Figure 2

A SNOWBALL MAKER

Snowball making is slow when carried on by hand. Where a thrower is employed in a snow fort, it becomes necessary to have a number of assistants in making the snowballs. The time of making these balls can be greatly reduced by the use of the snowball maker shown in the illustration.

The base consists of a board, 24 in. long by 6 ½ in. wide by 1 in. thick. A block of wood, A, is hollowed out in the center to make a depression in the shape of a hemisphere, 2 1/12 in. in diameter by 1 ¼ in. deep. This block is nailed to the base about 1 in. from one end. To make the dimensions come out right, fasten a block, B, 6 in. high—made of one or more pieces—at the other end of the base with its back edge 14 ½ in. from the center of the hemispherical depression. On top of this block, a 20-in.-long lever, C, is hinged. Another block, D, is made with a hemispherical depression like the block A, and fastened to the underside of the lever so that the depressions in both blocks will coincide. The lever end is shaped into a handle.

Two uprights, E, are fastened to the backside of the block A as guides for the lever C. A piece is fastened across their tops and a spring is attached between it and the lever. A curtain-roller spring will be suitable.

In making the balls, a bunch of snow is thrown into the lower depression and the lever brought down with considerable force.

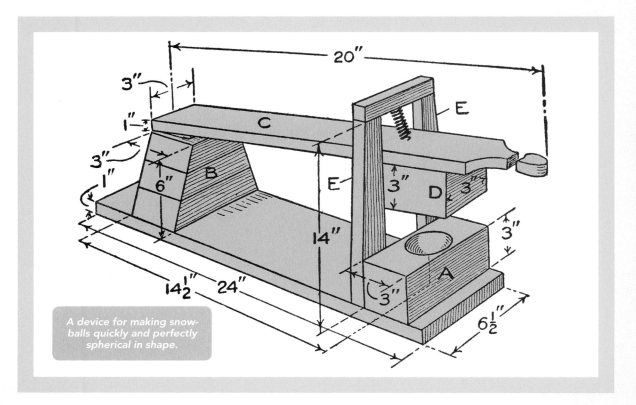

A device for making snowballs quickly and perfectly spherical in shape.

The snow fort with its infantry is not complete without the artillery. A set of mortars, or cannon, placed in the fort to hurl snowballs at the entrenched enemy makes the battle more real. A device to substitute for the cannon or a mortar can be easily constructed by any boy, and a few of these devices set in a snow fort will add greatly to the interest of the conflict.

The substitute—called a "snowball thrower"—consists of a base, A, with a standard, B, which stops the arm, C, controlled by the bar, D, when the trigger, E, is released. The tripping of the trigger is accomplished by the sloping end of D on the slanting end of the upright F, with their upper ends extending above the bar D, to prevent the latter from jumping out when it is released by the trigger.

The trigger E is tripped with the handle, H, connected to the piece, J, on which all the working parts are mounted. The upper end of the arm C has a piece, K, to which is attached a tin can, L, for holding the snowball to be thrown. A set of door springs, M, furnishes the force to throw the snowball.

All the parts are given dimensions, and if cut properly, they will fit together to make the thrower as illustrated.

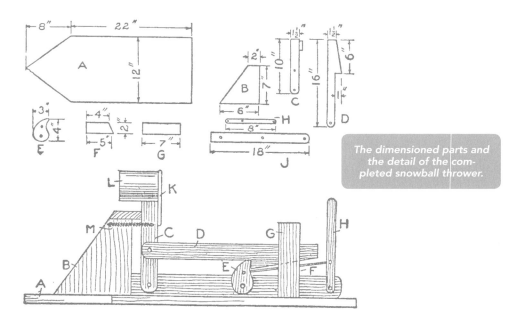

The dimensioned parts and the detail of the completed snowball thrower.

Cannonading a snow fort with the use of a snowball thrower.

101 THINGS THAT FLY

AERIAL AMUSEMENTS

TOYS THAT BOUND, LEAP, AND SOAR

MAKING A TOY CATAPULT

A 10-cent rat trap of the type shown in the drawing can easily be made into a marble-throwing catapult, the range of the missile being regulated by an adjustable stop. The trap is fastened to the edges of the ammunition box and the bait hook is removed. The stop is then bent from a strip of sheet metal and fastened to opposite edges of the trap as indicated. Two side arms that serve as braces for the stop are adjusted by means of a wire pin passing through holes in the stop and arms. The throwing arm should be made of ½ by ½ in. hardwood, about 10 in. long, although the length is best determined by trial. A small metal cup at the end of the arm provides a pocket for the ammunition. If desired, a trigger arrangement can be added. Flour tied in tissue paper may be used to make a realistic bomb because it gives off a smokelike puff when it strikes and is harmless. The longest throw the device is capable of will usually be attained when the stop is set at an angle of about 45 degrees.

RAT TRAP ----

ADJUSTABLE
STOP ----

RUBBER BAND
ON TRIGGER

AMMUNITION BOX

TINY ACROBAT ON TOY WINDMILL CUTS AMUSING CAPERS

Actuating a trapeze performer in a realistic manner, this wind toy will afford you many laughs, especially on a gusty day when the mill runs erratically. First get a base for the assembly, which can be a piece of hardwood or light channel iron. Fasten vertical pieces to it to carry the shaft and pulley that rotate the figure. Then provide simple bearings on the base for the airwheel shaft, which is a length of brass rod. Next, make up the wheel hub and pulley from hardwood, and drill it to take the shaft with a force fit, placing a washer between the hub and shaft bearing to prevent binding. Now you are ready for the wheel, which is a tin disk cut to resemble the wheel on a regular farm windmill. This is tacked to the hub. A tin tail vane is fastened to the rear of the base. Arms and legs of the figure are pivoted loosely to the body, while the arms are clamped tightly to the shaft.

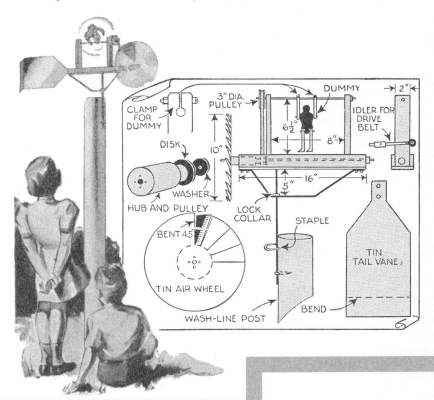

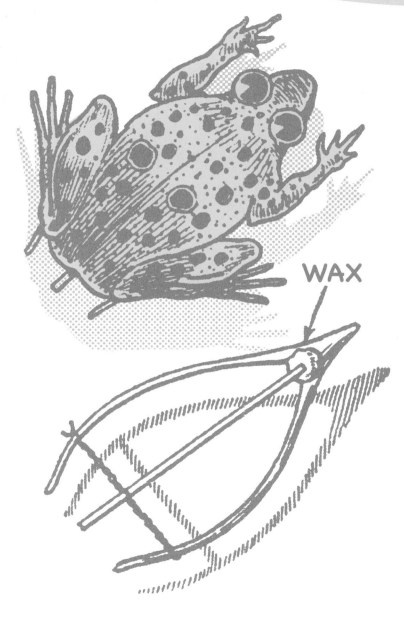

WAX

An entertaining little toy can be made from the wishbone of a fowl after it has been well cleaned and freed from flesh.

Take a piece of strong, thin string and double it, tying it securely to opposite sides of the wishbone about 1 in. from the ends, as in the drawing. Cut a strip of wood a little shorter than the bone, and make a circular notch about ½ in. from one end. Push the stick through the doubled string for about half its length, twist the string tightly by means of the stick, then pull the stick through until the notch is reached. From a piece of paper or thin cardboard, cut out the outline of a frog. Paint it to resemble the animal as nearly as possible, and paste this to one side of the wishbone. The only material now required is a piece of shoemaker's wax, which is placed on the underside of the bone, just where the free end of the stick will rest.

When a child wants to make the frog jump, she only needs to push the stick down and press the end into the wax. Place the frog on the table, and after a short while the toy will, all of a sudden, make a very lifelike leap as the end of the stick pulls away from the wax.

An East Indian toy, known as a "bandilore," is made from a piece of spool, about ½ or ¾ in. thick, and two tin disks, about 4 in. in diameter.

The section of spool is tacked between the two disks, exactly in the center. Tie one end of a 3- or 4-ft. length of stout cord to the spool. The bandilore is operated by winding the cord around the spool and holding the free end of the string in the hand. The toy is dropped and descends with great speed; just before the end of the cord is reached, the whole thing is given a quick upward jerk. This increases the speed and momentum of the disks so that the cord is wound in the opposite direction, and the bandilore climbs upward, the process being repeated as often as desired.

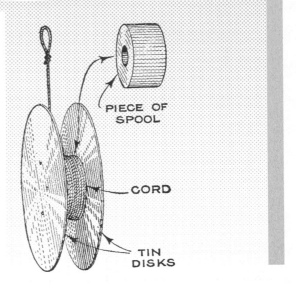

PIECE OF SPOOL

CORD

TIN DISKS

WOODEN MAN ON A STRING

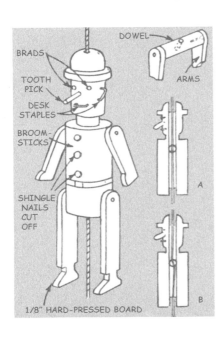

DOWEL

BRADS

TOOTH PICK

DESK STAPLES

BROOM-STICKS

ARMS

SHINGLE NAILS CUT OFF

A

B

1/8" HARD-PRESSED BOARD

When you know the secret command, this little man will slide down the string or stop when you tell him to. But for anyone else he'll only slide and refuse to stop until he reaches the bottom of the string. The real secret lies in the position of the dowel that fastens the two arms. There is a hole drilled in it, through which the string passes, and if this hole is aligned as shown in detail A, it will be impossible to stop the toy. However, if the hole is out of alignment, as shown in detail B, the man will slide when there is little tension on the string and stop when it is pulled tight. Care must be taken to be sure that the dowel is a tight fit in the body for the toy to work properly. The man is carved from a broomstick and he has hard-pressed-board arms and legs. Shingle nails, staples, brads, and a toothpick serve as features and decoration. Gaily colored enamels will give the toy an attractive appearance.

MAKE PAPER BALLOONS

This project involves using flammable materials to create a miniature hot-air balloon, and because of the danger of fire, the balloon should be ignited and flown only under the supervision of adults and with the appropriate safety precautions, including a fire extinguisher. The balloon should be flown only over water.

This type of balloon, made spherical or designed like the regular aeronaut's hot-air balloon, is the best kind to make. Those having an odd or unusual shape will not make good ascensions, and in most cases, the paper will catch fire from the torch and burn before they have flown very far. The following description is for making a tissue-paper balloon about 6 ft. high.

The paper may be selected in several colors. The gores cut from these and pasted in alternately will produce a pretty array of colors when the balloon is in flight. The shape of a good balloon is shown in *Figure 1*. The gores for a 6-ft. balloon should be about 8 ft. long or about one-third longer than the height of the balloon. The widest part of each gore is 16 in. The widest place should be

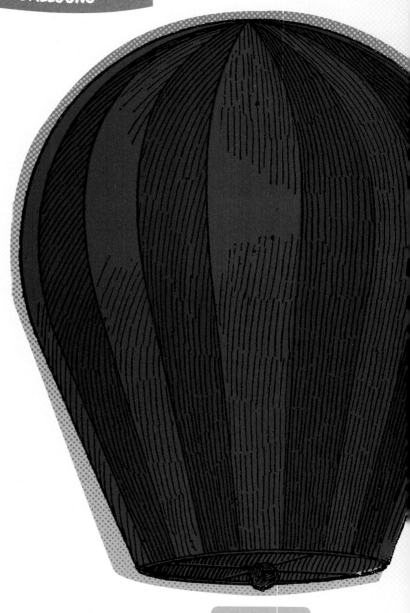

Figure 1:
Paper balloon.

53 1/2 in. from the bottom end, or a little over halfway from the bottom to the top. The bottom of the gore is one-third the width of the widest point. The dimensions and shape of each gore are shown in *Figure 2*.

The balloon is made up of 13 gores pasted together, using about 1/2-in. lap on the edges. Any good paste will do—one that is made up of a well-cooked mixture of flour and water will serve the purpose. If the gores have been put together correctly, the pointed ends will close up the top entirely and the wider bottom ends will leave an opening about 20 in. in diameter. A light wood hoop having the same diameter as the opening is pasted to the bottom end of the gores. Two cross wires are fastened to the hoop, as shown in *Figure 3*. These are to hold the wick ball, *Figure 4*, so that it will hang as shown in *Figure 5*. The wick ball is made by winding wicking around a wire, with the wire ends bent into hooks as shown.

The balloon is filled with hot air in a manner similar to that used with the ordinary cloth balloon. A small trench or fireplace is made of brick with a chimney over which the mouth of the paper balloon is placed. Use fuel that will make heat with very little smoke. Hold the balloon so it will not catch fire from the flames coming out of the chimney. Have some alcohol ready to pour on the wick ball, saturating it thoroughly. When the balloon is filled with hot air, carry it away from the fireplace, attach the wick ball to the cross wires, and light it under the supervision of an adult.

In starting the balloon on its flight, take care that it leaves the ground as nearly upright as possible.

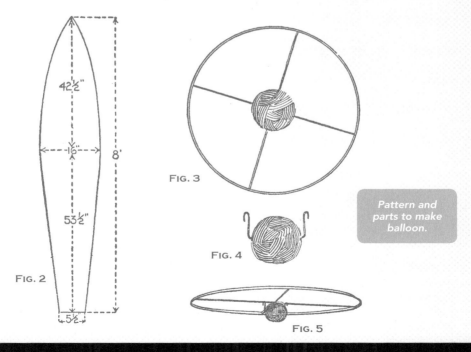

FIG. 2

42 1/2"

16"

8'

53 1/2"

5 1/2"

FIG. 3

FIG. 4

FIG. 5

Pattern and parts to make balloon.

TOSSING CONTESTS

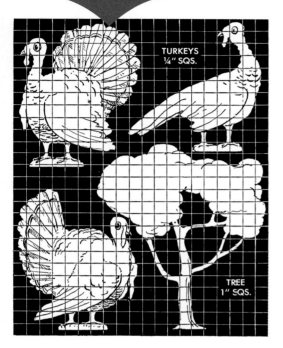

TURKEYS ¼" SQS.

TREE 1" SQS.

TURKEY-HUNT GAME

Bag a turkey if you will, but the consequence written on its back may have you scouring the town for a red horsehair or walking upstairs on your hands. The game can be a riot at a party, depending on the originality of the penalties. One turkey wins a prize, but the players don't know which one. The backstop is made of stiff cardboard and painted to represent sky and landscape. The trees and turkeys also can be made of cardboard, but they will be more durable if jigsawed from thin plywood. Standards are fitted to the various targets, while tabs permit some of the birds to roost in the trees. A bow is shaped from a piece of bamboo fish pole and strung with a length of fishline. Darts are made of ⅛-in. dowel, tipped with a cartridge shell. Feathers are lashed to the opposite end with silk thread and cement.

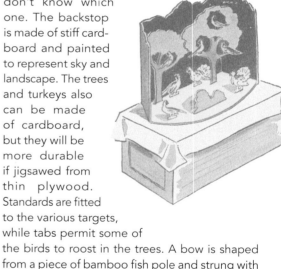

LONG BAMBOO JOINT CUT AS INDICATED
¼"　⅛"

LIGHT FISHLINE

.22-CAL. FIRED SHELL
⅛" DOWEL　SILK THREAD
STRIP OF FEATHER

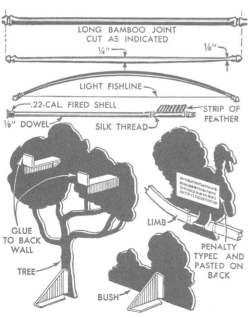

GLUE TO BACK WALL

TREE

BUSH

LIMB

PENALTY TYPED AND PASTED ON BACK

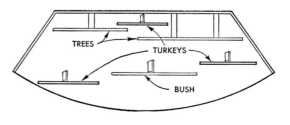

TREES
TURKEYS
BUSH

THROW BEAN BAGS FOR FUN

This indoor game looks easy at first sight, but when you try it you'll find it's a game of skill that will hold you for hours at a time. It's something like pitching horseshoes, except that the score is made—or lost—by tossing small beanbags through holes cut in a vertical panel. The winning number of points may be decided upon by the opposing teams and the score of the individual players recorded on the scoreboard provided.

After passing through the holes in the panel, the bags slide down to the bottom and collect behind a rectangular opening from which they are easily removed. Note that when the box is set up, the weight rests on the "feet" cut in the lower end of the panel and on the braces. The latter are of a length to tilt the box back slightly so that it stands firmly. The cloth bags, four for each player, measure about 3 ½ by 5 in. and are filled about three-fourths full of dry beans or clean pebbles of uniform size.

HARDW

¼" HO

Requiring only a floating court and two sets of wooden disks, all of which can be made n a few hours, "skip scotch" is an action-packed game that provides real fun at the beach. After the court has been anchored in the water 60 ft. from the shoreline, each player attempts to skip four disks into the highest-scoring section of the court. The first player to score 18 points is the winner of the game.

The court sections are numbered as shown in the detail, the front, or triangular, section having the highest number of points. One point is subtracted from the player's score for each disk that misses the court, and disks that come to rest on the framework are not counted. These rules, of course, are merely suggested ones and they can be altered as desired. The wooden framework is made as shown and, after the top has been painted white so it can be seen easily, the entire court is given a coat of spar varnish.

Small convex disks can be made of hardwood, or larger, flat disks of waterproof plywood can be used. One set of disks is painted yellow and the other set red, all of them being given a final coat of spar varnish. Before painting, the centers of the disks are drilled so they can be strung on a length of sash cord or clothesline for carrying.

Anchors attached to the front and rear of the court hold it in position, and their lines should be as short as possible to keep the court from swinging. Cans filled with concrete will provide anchors. If the game is to be carried in a car, the court can be hinged to fold compactly or made in two or more separate sections that can be quickly hooked or screwed together at the beach and later taken apart in a few minutes for carrying.

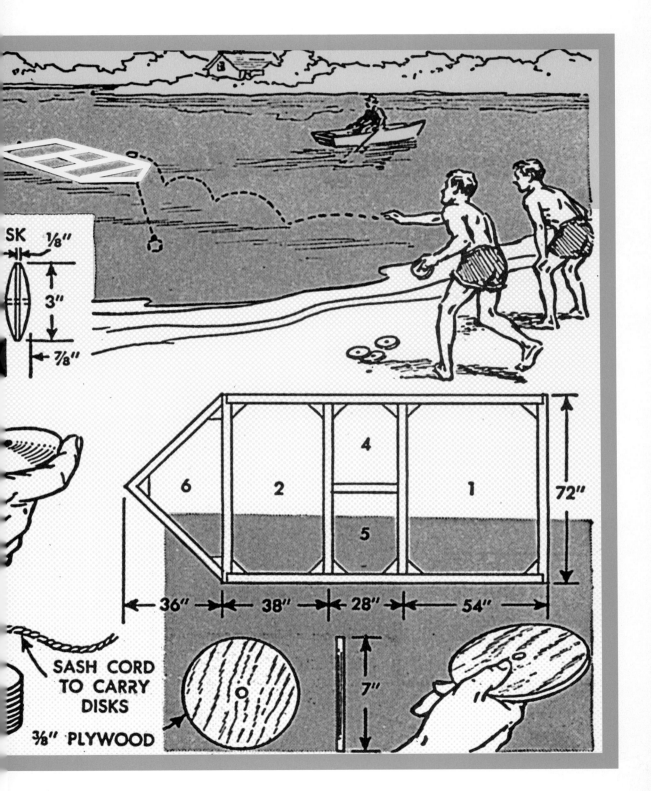

SK   1/8"

3"

7/8"

4

6   2   1

5

72"

36"   38"   28"   54"

SASH CORD
TO CARRY
DISKS

3/8" PLYWOOD

7"

"SWING BALL"

"**B**owling" on a tabletop requires skill, provides plenty of action, and gives the entire family wholesome diversion on long winter evenings. You count strikes and spares, as in regular bowling, but you play with a suspended ball, manipulation of which requires some of the precision of billiards. The pins are turned on a lathe and the game board is arranged to fold compactly, forming a box in which all the loose parts can be stored. Or, if desired, a game board that is portable, but not folding, can be provided.

The ten pins and their arrangement is similar to the conventional bowling set-up,

except that the triangular bank of pins points away from the player instead of facing the player, and is located on one side of the center line. The suspended ball is four times heavier than a single pin and crashes through the bank of pins the same way as a bowling ball does on an alley, after which it returns to the hand of the player. The ball must be swung in an elliptical path, hitting the pins on the return swing. It is this part of the game that gives rise to some interesting calculations. Regardless of which point the ball begins its course, or how wide the ellipse traveled, the distances *A* and *B*, as shown in *Figure 7*, are always the same.

In the game, you follow rules of conventional bowling. Players alternate, swinging the ball twice at each turn unless all pins are knocked down with the first swing, which is a strike. Knocking all the pins down in two swings gives you a "spare." When a player makes a strike, she counts the score plus the ten of the strike plus the number of pins made in her next two swings. In the case of a spare, she adds the ten of the spare to the score, plus the number of pins made on her next swing. Two swings—unless a strike is made—constitute a frame, and ten frames make a line, or game. If a pin is knocked over on the forward swing, if a

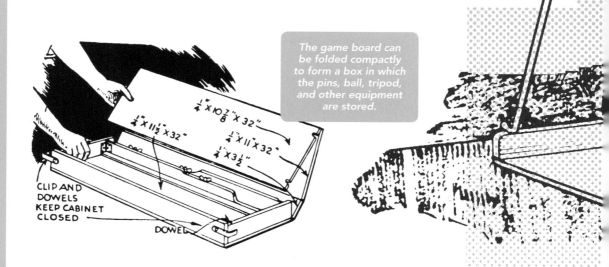

The game board can be folded compactly to form a box in which the pins, ball, tripod, and other equipment are stored.

CLIP AND DOWELS KEEP CABINET CLOSED

DOWEL

$\frac{1}{4}" \times 10\frac{7}{8}" \times 32"$

$\frac{1}{4}" \times 11\frac{1}{2}" \times 32"$

$\frac{1}{4}" \times 11" \times 32"$

$\frac{1}{4}" \times 3\frac{1}{2}"$

This table-bowling game, in which a swinging ball is brought to bear upon a bank of ten pins, has many points in common with the usual bowling game.

CONT

player fails to catch the ball on its return swing, if the pins are missed entirely, or if the ball strikes the leg of the tripod, it is deemed a "gutter ball" and constitutes a scoreless play in which any pins that may have been knocked over do not count. Regular bowling score sheets can be purchased at amusement supply stores, or one can be permanently painted on a chalkboard.

The game table is made up of four panels of ¼-in. plywood or hard-pressed board. These panels, laid cut in their respective positions, are covered with a piece of 8-oz. canvas that is glued on. After the glue has set, the surplus cloth at the edges is trimmed away and the end piece and side pieces are mounted on the baseboard with wood screws, the side pieces forming the end of the box when the game board is closed. Hinged to these stationary side pieces are two extensions that

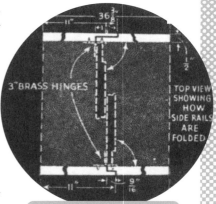

The circular detail shows how two hinged rails, which form part of the sides of the game board, are folded together, collapsing it to form a box.

complete the sides of the game board when it is in use. These are held rigidly to the edge of the end panel that comes directly under the tripod, by means of bolts and wing nuts—two on one extension and one on the other. Notches in the edge of the end panels permit the bolts to be slipped in place readily. Besides serving the purpose of attaching the extensions rigidly, the bolts also hold the feet of the tripod. When the game board is to be folded, the bolts are loosened, the tripod is removed, and the extensions are folded together. This way, they will be next to each other, against a cross batten that is screwed down permanently and bears the following instruction: "Gather All Toppled Pins Back on This Slat

Details of assembly and arrangement showing the simplicity of construction. In playing, the pins knocked down by each swing are gathered into the space behind the slat that serves as a deadline.

Before Making Second Swing."
Other details on the construction and assembly of the game
board, such as the clip-and-dowel
arrangement for holding the box
closed, can be obtained by going
over the drawings. The centerline
and the ball suspension spot are
marked with black ink or paint.

Now for the accessories to the
game: The belly of the pins is 1 $\frac{7}{16}$
in. in diameter, so they can be
turned readily from 1 $\frac{1}{2}$ x 1 $\frac{1}{2}$-in.
stock. Maple is particularly recom-
mended, but beech, mahogany, or
Australian gum can also be used.
The ball is turned from maple or
lignum-vitae, although a billiard
ball also serves the purpose. When
a maple ball is used, it is heavily

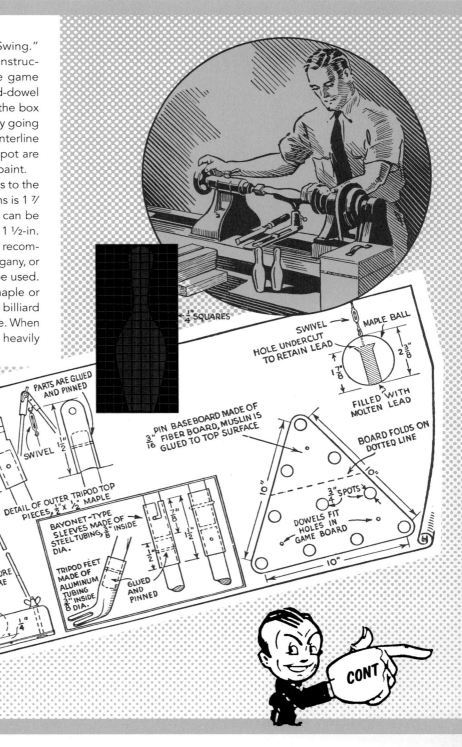

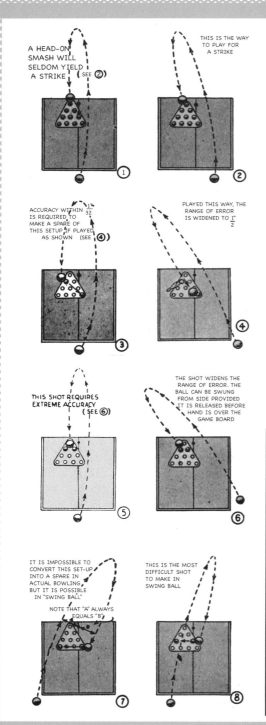

A HEAD-ON SMASH WILL SELDOM YIELD A STRIKE (SEE ②)

THIS IS THE WAY TO PLAY FOR A STRIKE

① ②

ACCURACY WITHIN $\frac{1''}{32}$ IS REQUIRED TO MAKE A SPARE OF THIS SETUP IF PLAYED AS SHOWN (SEE ④)

PLAYED THIS WAY, THE RANGE OF ERROR IS WIDENED TO $\frac{1''}{2}$

③ ④

THIS SHOT REQUIRES EXTREME ACCURACY (SEE ⑥)

THE SHOT WIDENS THE RANGE OF ERROR. THE BALL CAN BE SWUNG FROM SIDE PROVIDED IT IS RELEASED BEFORE HAND IS OVER THE GAME BOARD

⑤ ⑥

IT IS IMPOSSIBLE TO CONVERT THIS SET-UP INTO A SPARE IN ACTUAL BOWLING, BUT IT IS POSSIBLE IN "SWING BALL"

NOTE THAT "A" ALWAYS EQUALS "B"

THIS IS THE MOST DIFFICULT SHOT TO MAKE IN SWING BALL

⑦ ⑧

weighted with metal, as shown in one of the details. The hole is enlarged at its base to retain the metal, which is poured when it is barely above its melting point, in order to avoid scorching the wood. The construction of the tripod is clearly illustrated. Bayonet-type sleeves are necessary on the legs, because the oscillations of the ball put a strain on the legs that would work straight ferrules loose. A swivel at the top of the tripod holds a length of picture wire from which the ball is suspended, another swivel being provided at the ball end. The pin baseboard folds as indicated by the dotted lines in one of the details. It is fitted with three dowels that are glued in place and project on the underside so that they can be set into holes drilled in the surface of the game board. This assures the correct position of the pins at all times.

Now, let's play swing ball. First, the tripod legs must be adjusted to bring the ball directly over the suspension spot, and the wire adjusted to hold the ball ¼ in. off the game board. *Figures 1* to *8* illustrate a few of the swings or "shots." Strangely, a strike will seldom result from a head-on hit of the kingpin. *Figure 2* shows the more scientific way to go after a strike. Two-pin shots will crop up constantly in the play, and the player

most adept at making them, thereby recording a spare, is the girl who will win the most games, other factors being equal. Careful playing, with application to the technique of making the spares count, will aid materially in shooting a higher score.

A SNAKE GAME

Ask any Canadian Native American what a snow snake is, and he will tell you that it is a piece of twisted wood, such as wild grape vine, about 5 or 6 ft. long, and 1 in. or more in thickness, stripped of its bark and polished. It is grasped with one hand in the center and given a strong forward throw at the tail end by the other hand, while at the same time the hold in the center is loosened. With a hard bottom and about 1 in. or more of light snow on top—ideal conditions for playing the game—the snake will travel for long distances when thrown by an expert. To a novice, seeing the snake traveling along at a rapid speed, raising and lowering its head as the wood vibrates from side to side, its resemblance to the real reptile is perfect.

When the Native Americans have tests of skill with the snake, they make tracks through the snow by drawing a log in it. Sometimes as many as a dozen tracks are made side by side, and a dozen snakes are sent along at once. The one who makes his snake emerge from the end of the track first the most times out of a certain number of throws takes the prize. The trick of throwing the snake is not at all hard to acquire, and it makes for an exciting game.

Throwing the snow snake in tracks made through the snow with a log. Each player tries to get his snake first out at the end of the track more times than his opponents.

A BUCKET-BALL GAME

This is a new indoor game that follows out in principle a regular game of baseball. It is an exciting and interesting pastime. And while a certain amount of skill is required to score runs, a person who cannot play the regular game can score as many runs, and as often as the best players in the professional leagues.

Anyone who is just a little handy with tools can make the necessary parts for this game. The tools required are a hammer and a saw. The materials consist of some finishing nails; three strips of wood, 6 ft. long, 2 in. wide, and 1 in. thick; two strips, 18 in. long, 4 in. wide, and 1 in. thick; four strips, 24 in. long, 2 in. wide, and 1 in. thick; two strips, 18 in. long, 2 in. wide, and 1 in. thick; two blocks, 4 in.

square and 1 in. thick; and four wood buckets.

A frame is built up as shown, 6 ft. long, 18 in. wide, and 24 in. high, without a back. One of the long pieces is fastened to the bottoms of the buckets as shown, spacing the latter equally on the length of the piece. This piece is then set in notches cut in the blocks of wood at an angle of 45 degrees. These blocks are fastened to the upper crosspieces at the ends of the frame. The upper part of the buckets rest on the upper front piece of the frame.

The rules for playing the game are as follows: Three baseballs are used. The players stand about 10 ft. away and in front of the buckets. Each player, or side, is permitted to throw only three balls

an inning, irrespective of the number of runs scored. Any kind of delivery is permitted, but an underhand throw will be found most successful. The buckets are numbered from 1 to 4, and represent, respectively, one-, two-, and three-base hits, and home runs. The one in which the ball stays designates the run.

Plays are figured as in a regular ballgame. For instance, if a ball should stay in bucket *No. 2* and the next in bucket *No. 3*, the first man would be forced home, counting one run, and leaving one man on third base. If the next ball stays in bucket *No. 4*, the man on third base is forced home, as well as the one who scored the home run, making three runs for that inning. The runs should be scored as made.

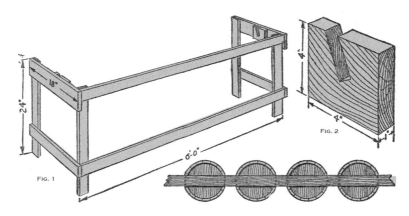

FIG. 1

FIG. 2

The frame is made up without a back, to hold the buckets at an angle that makes it difficult to toss the ball so that it will stay in any one of them.

The player must throw the ball so that it will enter and stay in one of the buckets, which designates the base hits by the number in its bottom.

FIG. 3

FIG. 4

Parlor cue alley is really a game of bowling except that it is played on a small raised board. Instead of throwing the balls by hand, an ordinary billiard cue is used, the balls being about 1 ¼ in. in diameter. The automatic feature of this new game saves the time usually required to set up the pins, and assures that they will be set absolutely true each time.

To build this alley, first procure three planed boards. Use hardwood even though it is more difficult to work. Two of the boards should be 10 ft. long, 9 in. wide, and ½ in. thick, and the other 10 ft. long, 15 in.

wide, and ½ in. thick. Place the first two boards side by side and fasten them with cleats, the first cleat being placed 18 in. from the end to be used for the pins. The cleats should be of ¾- or ⅞-in. material and cut as long as the upper board is wide, or 15 in. These are placed on top of the lower boards, or between the two. By placing the first one 18 in. from the end, clearance is obtained for the trap A. The other board is placed on the cleats and fastened,

after it has been centrally located, with screws from the underside. The screws must not come through or the surface of the upper board marred in any way that might prevent the balls from rolling freely. The difference in width of the lower board

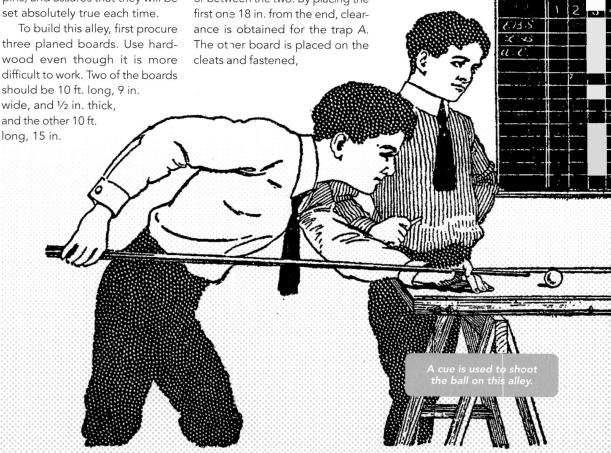

A cue is used to shoot the ball on this alley.

and the upper one provides a 1 ½-in. clearance on each side as grooves for the return of the balls.

Enclose the alley with boards, 3 in. wide and ½ in. thick, to the point B, and from there around the pin end with boards, 6 in. wide.

The upper board should be cut to such a length that a space of 2 in. at the end C will be provided. Into this space is fitted a block of wood, about ⅞ in. thick, with its upper surface slightly pitched toward the sides of the alley to start the balls back to the front of the board. From the ends of this block, two 1 ½-in.-wide strips are fitted into the side grooves, from D to E. They should be set on an incline, to return the ball after each shot.

The location of each pin is marked on the end of the upper board. Small holes are drilled just large enough to allow pieces of stout cord, like a fish line, to

pass through freely. The pins are made of hardwood and are carefully balanced; one end should not be heavier than the other. The lower end of each pin is drilled to make a recess, F, in which the cord is fastened with a screw or nail. Holes are bored through the bottom board, ⅜ in. in diameter, to correspond to the 10 small holes made through the upper one. Lead weights of about 2 oz. are fitted in the holes and attached to the strings from the pins. The ends of the weights should extend about ½ in. from the underside of the alley.

Attach a board, 18 in. square, with hinges to the end of the alley so that it will hang under the weights. A stout cord is run along the underside of the alley to the

front end through screw eyes, and attached to the swinging board. By letting the board swing down, the weights are released and they draw the pins into a standing position, accurately set for the next break. When set, the line is drawn, and the swinging board pushes the weights up and releases the pins.

The balls used are made of hardwood. If it is not possible to make them, they can be purchased from a toy store. They are 1 ¼ in. in diameter. Each player has three shots. The ball is placed on the spot G and shot with a billiard cue, the object being to knock down as many pins as possible. The score is kept as in bowling.

Horses can be made of metal and wood, as shown, for holding the alley at the proper height. The alley can be used on a large table, but horses are more convenient.

The alley board with its attachments.

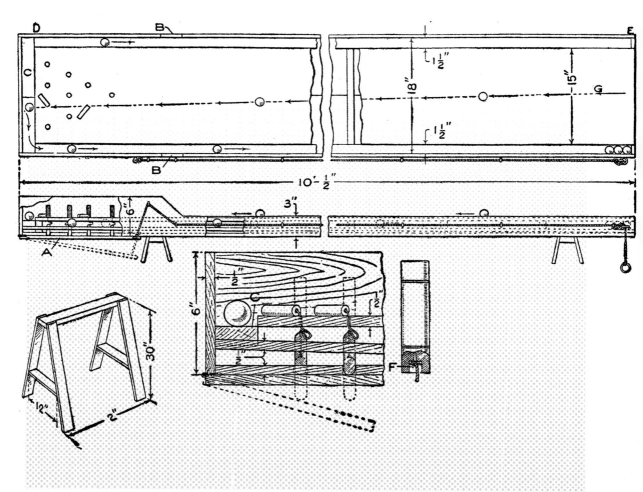

101 THINGS THAT FLY

Especially suitable for indoor play, this game of horseshoes is ideal entertainment for children on rainy days. Because the "shoes" are rubber, being cut from an old car tire, they cannot scratch the floor and help keep the game a quiet one. The stakes are provided by driving two clothespins or wooden pegs into blocks of ¾-in. wood, 10 or 12 in. square.

AN INDOOR BASEBALL GAME

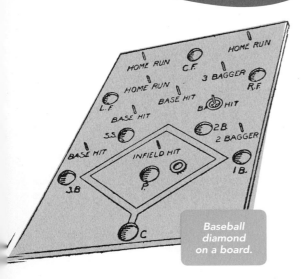

Baseball diamond on a board.

An indoor game of baseball may be played on a board 5 ft. long and 4 ft. wide. A diamond is laid off at one end of the board and pins representing the hits are attached to the board so they will project above the surface. The locations of the players are designated by holes bored partway in the wood with an expansive bit. These holes should be large enough to receive the rings easily. The rings may be gaskets or they may be made of rope, and should have an inside diameter of about 3 in.

Only two people can play this game. The distance from the board to the thrower may be from 10 to 100 ft., according to the size of the room. This distance should be marked and each thrower stands at the same place.

If the ring is thrown over one of the "base-hit" or "two-bagger" pegs, it shows the number of bases secured. Throwing a ring over one of the "home run" pegs means a score, of course. The "infield hit" secures a base. If the ring slips into a hole, that counts as one out. A player must throw until he has three outs. The score is kept for the runs made.

SHOOTING TARGETS

A RECORDING ANNUNCIATOR TARGET

Figure 1

In rifle practice, it is often desirable to provide a target that will indicate to the marksman when the bull's-eye is struck. The device shown in the sketch, arranged behind an ordinary card target, has given satisfactory results on a private range and can easily be adapted to other uses.

Referring to *Figure 1*, A indicates a wooden base, 4 by 8 by ½ in., on which is mounted a strap hinge, *B*, 6 ½ in. long, by means of a block, 1 ³⁄₈ in. high. An opening, *C*, 1 ½ in. in diameter, is provided in the base. A plate, *D*, 1 ³⁄₄ in. square, is riveted to the strap hinge opposite to the opening. An electromagnet, *E*, obtained from an electric bell, is mounted upon the base under the small end of the hinge. A standard, *F*, provided with a cross arm, *G*, is secured upon the base between the opening and the magnet. A thumbscrew with a locknut extends through the cross arm, engaging the rear side of the strap hinge, and permits an adjustment of d stance between the core of the magnet and the surface of the hinge. A bell or buzzer, *H*, is connected as indicated, through the battery circuit. The electromagnet is connected through the battery and push button *J*.

The strap hinge normally rests against the electromagnet. The force of any projectile passing through the opening against the plate closes the bell circuit and indicates to the marksman that the bull's-eye has been hit. By closing the magnetic circuit, the strap hinge is drawn again into normal position and the bell circuit is broken. *Figure 2* shows a front view of the circuit-closing device. The device may be mounted in any suitable box, as suggested in *Figure 3*. The front of the box is covered with sheet metal, ¹⁄₁₆ in. thick, and the standard target card is mounted thereon.

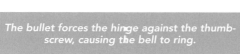

The bullet forces the hinge against the thumbscrew, causing the bell to ring.

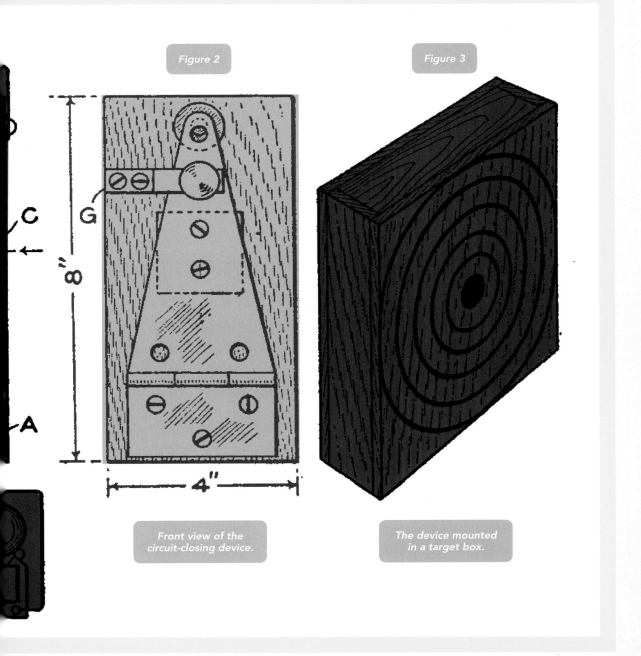

Figure 2

Front view of the circuit-closing device.

Figure 3

The device mounted in a target box.

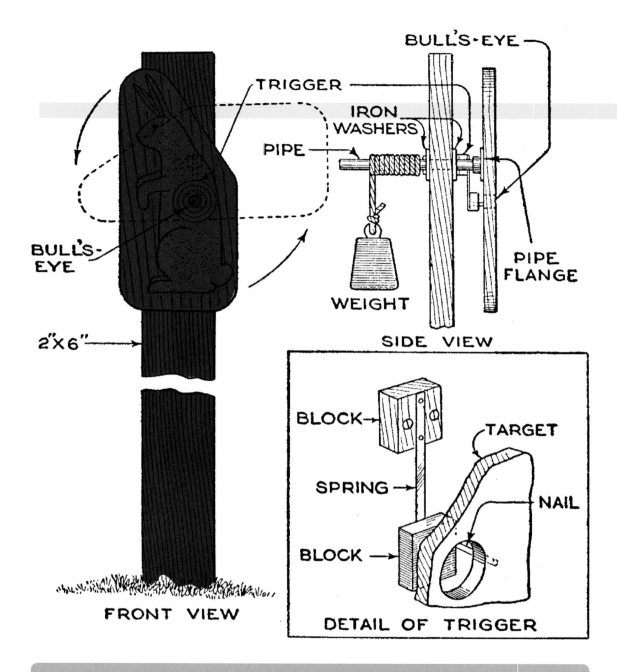

TRIGGER

BULL'S-EYE

IRON WASHERS

PIPE

BULL'S-EYE

2"X6"

FRONT VIEW

WEIGHT

SIDE VIEW

PIPE FLANGE

BLOCK

SPRING

BLOCK

TARGET

NAIL

DETAIL OF TRIGGER

Whenever the marksman makes a bull's-eye on this target, the "bunny" makes a complete somersault, and turns again to an upright position ready for another shot.

THE SOMERSAULTING "BUNNY" TARGET

The somersaulting "bunny" target shown in the drawing is intended for target practice with bow and arrow. But, by substituting sheet-iron parts for the wooden ones described, it may be used as well for small-caliber rifle practice.

The rabbit is outlined on a 10-by-24-in. board with the rings and bull's-eye of the target a trifle off center to the right; the bull's-eye is formed by drilling a 1 ½-in. hole through the board.

A 2-by-6-in. post is used for supporting the target, which is mounted on a shaft so as to revolve freely. A piece of gas pipe, about 12 in. long, will answer for the shaft. This is inserted through a hole drilled in the post and is attached to the back of the target with a floor flange. A washer on each side of the post, together with cotter pins driven through holes in the shaft, serve to maintain the proper space between the post and target for operation of the trigger.

The trigger is made by fastening two blocks of wood to the opposite ends and sides of a piece of spring steel. One of the blocks is nailed to the post in such a position as to bring the other block directly behind the bull's-eye block and, by bearing against a nail in the back of the target, to hold the rabbit vertically until the trigger is released by a properly placed shot.

The somersaulting effect is produced by the weight arrangement shown in the drawing. A piece of stout twine is wound around the projecting end of the shaft, behind the post, and a weight is attached to the free end. The target remains stationary until a lucky shot springs the trigger. The weight then unwinds the rope, and the rabbit makes a complete revolution, the nail striking the block again and stopping the target when it is in an upright position.

From 10 to 20 bull's-eyes may be recorded by the somersaulting bunny before it has to be rewound, depending on the number of turns of rope around the shaft.

SHOOTING GALLERY FOR TOY PISTOLS

Skill in shooting toy pistols, blowguns, and similar harmless weapons that use peas, marbles, or wooden darts for ammunition can be easily honed by practicing on a target of the type shown in the drawing. Clothespins, spools, and some wire are about the only materials required. The clothespins are placed on a stiff wire or small rod with a spool between each pair. The wire is then fitted in a box, as shown. In back of the clothespins and a little above their lower ends is a second wire that holds them upright. This wire should be placed so that the pins will lean forward a little. When these targets are knocked over by an expert—or lucky—shot, they are caught by the pin-setting rod at the back. This rod is bent from a piece of stiff wire and is held horizontally by a rubber band. When all the targets have been knocked over, or after each marksman's turn is over, the pins are reset by a pull on the cord tied to the pin-setting rod. If desired, the clothespins can be painted and designated by numbers.

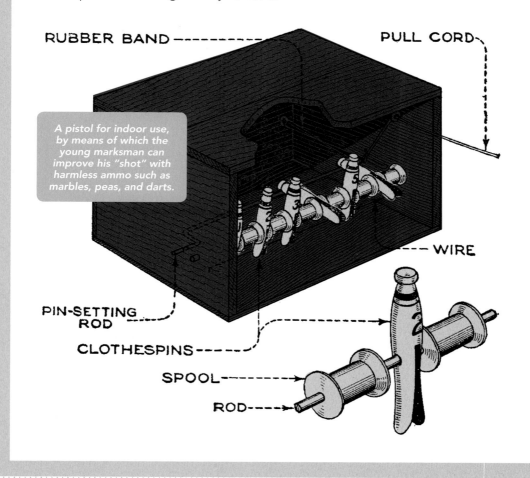

RUBBER BAND

PULL CORD

A pistol for indoor use, by means of which the young marksman can improve his "shot" with harmless ammo such as marbles, peas, and darts.

WIRE

PIN-SETTING ROD

CLOTHESPINS

SPOOL

ROD

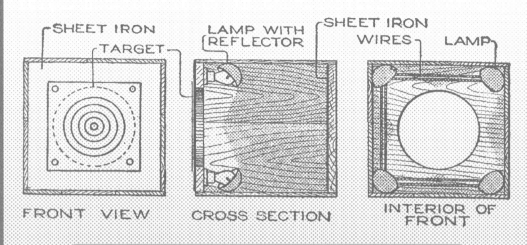

SHEET IRON
TARGET

LAMP WITH
REFLECTOR

SHEET IRON
WIRES   LAMP

FRONT VIEW   CROSS SECTION   INTERIOR OF FRONT

The location of hits is recorded by a beam of light streaming through the hole shot in the paper target.

The joys of target practice are often hampered by the delays in the settlement of hits. It takes time and is annoying to be constantly advancing to the target to examine it. To do away with this, an illuminated target was constructed that enables the shooter to locate every hit without leaving his post. To make the device, a square wooden box of convenient size is obtained. In one side of this, cut a round hole as large as the largest ring on the targets used. The side opposite this is fitted with a piece of sheet iron to stop the bullets. Paint this iron and the interior white. Inside the box, arrange four electric lights so their rays will be thrown on the hole, as shown. Candles may be used, if necessary. The lamps must be out of range of the bullets that hit the target, and protected by an iron plate. The targets are painted on thin paper and fastened over the front of the hole. The lights are turned on while shooting. Each shot punctures the paper, and the light streaming through the hole will show the location of the hit.

101 THINGS THAT FLY

SWINGS THAT SAIL

MAKE A VENETIAN SWING

The Venetian or gondola swing is an old enough feature of amusement in public parks, but it is seldom used in private grounds, although it is not by any means hard to build. It is an ideal yard toy for a little girl and her friends—one that can in time be handed down to younger siblings. Built properly, it will stand any amount of abuse, and the high sides of the gondola, or car, make it safe for the little ones. The design shown in the illustration has, moreover, an interesting feature that makes it a prime favorite with the children. The sides of the gondola have four disks painted to represent faces, the eyes of which roll and the tongues loll from side to side as the car swings.

The construction is simple. A pattern for the sides of the car, which may be of any size desired, is given in the detail drawing. The ends are perfectly circular, and four disks of the same size as the ends are cut at the same time, from the same material. Four smaller disks, about 3 or 4 in. less in diameter, may also be cut. A large disk is fitted to each end, as shown, by means of bolts, with spacers slipped over them so as to leave room for the smaller disks to work between. The outer disks may then be laid aside, the smaller ones centered on the ends of the car sides, and pivoted to them, either with heavy screws or with bolts. After this, the position of the tongues may be marked on them. Two holes for the eyes are then bored in each of the larger disks, the location and length of the tongue slots or mouths marked, and the disks slotted.

The tongues are simply strips of flat iron, bent and screwed to the inner disks and painted red. The eyes on the disks are merely large black dots. When the swing is operated, the inner disks swing from side to side, the length of the swing being governed by the length of the mouth slots.

The car is suspended by four $\frac{3}{8}$- or $\frac{1}{2}$-in. iron rods. These are flattened at the bottom, bent to conform to the shape of the car, and screwed in place. They are also flattened at the top, bent, drilled, and bolted to the cut-off ends of two old auto-engine connecting rods. These are mounted on a shaft of proper size, secured by means of eyebolts to the crossbar of the swing frame. Collars should be provided at each end of the shaft and on either side of the connecting rods, to prevent endwise motion.

The frame needs no description, but the method of operating the swing may perhaps be new to many. The top board of the frame cross-member is made as wide and as stout as possible, and from it two ropes are hung, in the center, reaching down to the car. The ropes are crossed, and the occupants off the seats, by pulling the ropes alternately, set it in motion and keep it going. Of course, the farther apart the ropes are at the top, the easier it is to start and operate the swing. So an additional length of 2-by-4-in. lumber may be bolted at right angles to the upper frame cross-member, as indicated by the dotted lines in the detail, and the ropes attached to the ends of this.

When the swing is operated, the eyes on its sides roll and the tongues loll from side to side in a realistic manner.

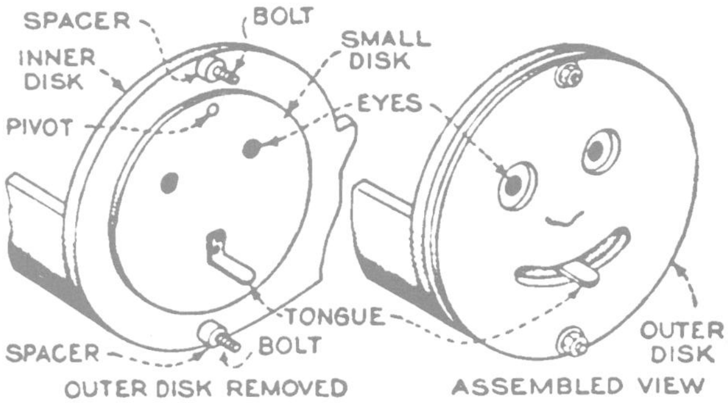

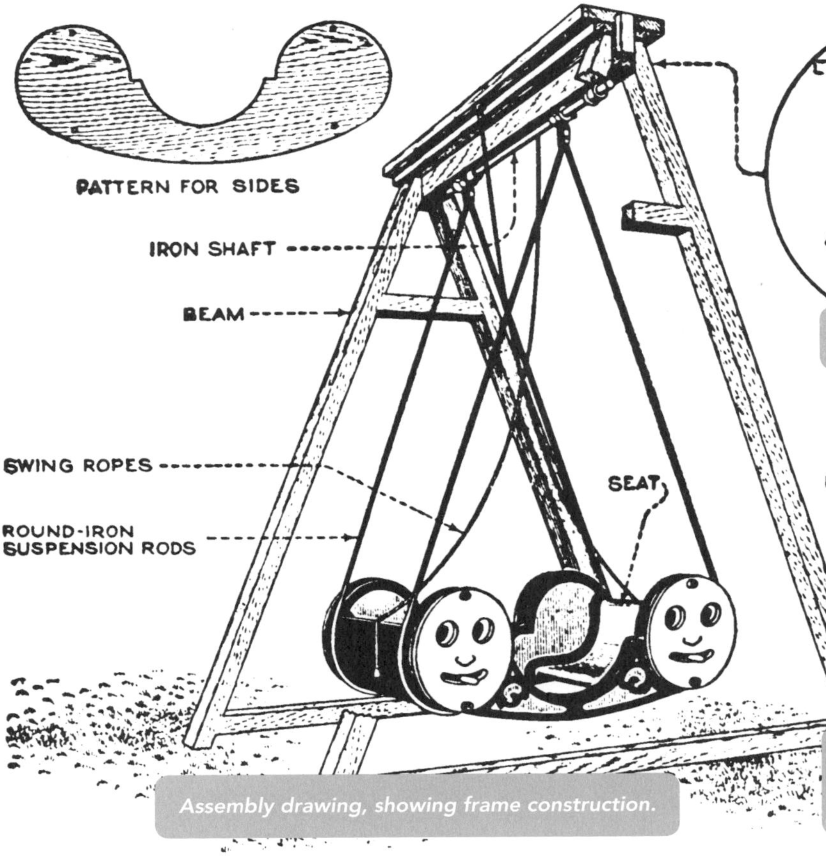

SPACER
INNER DISK
PIVOT
BOLT
SMALL DISK
EYES

SPACER
TONGUE BOLT
OUTER DISK REMOVED

OUTER DISK
ASSEMBLED VIEW

PATTERN FOR SIDES

IRON SHAFT

BEAM

SWING ROPES

ROUND-IRON SUSPENSION RODS

SEAT

Assembly drawing, showing frame construction.

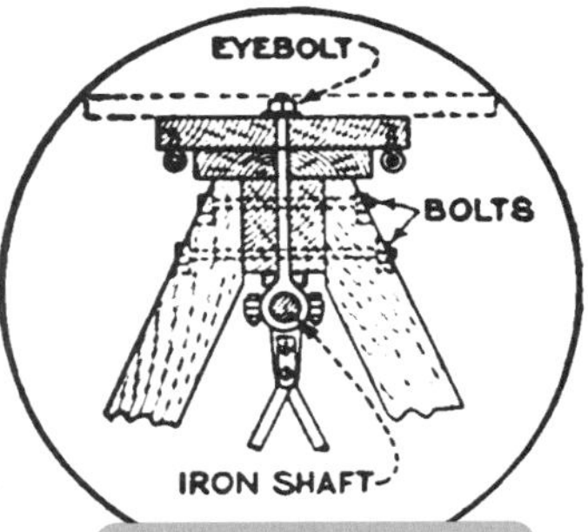

EYEBOLT

BOLTS

IRON SHAFT

Detail of suspension.

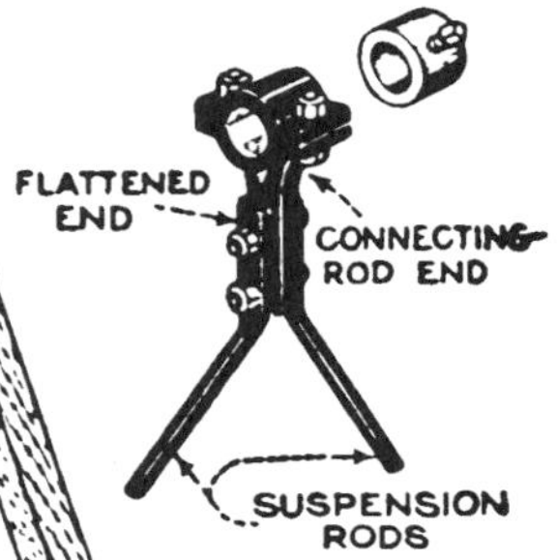

FLATTENED END

CONNECTING ROD END

SUSPENSION RODS

Method of fastening suspension rods to connecting-rod end.

Suspended from vertical rocker arms, which in turn are cushioned with discarded auto-spring leaves, this novel swing gives the passenger a long, undulated slide. The stop blocks against which the springs operate can be spaced for the smoothest action. The wood need not even be surfaced, but below the ground it should be treated with creosote to prevent decay. The axis for the wig-wag supports consists of large machine bolts, with a section of brass tubing for a bearing.

"FLYING-HORSE" SWING HAS NOVEL DUAL CONTROLS

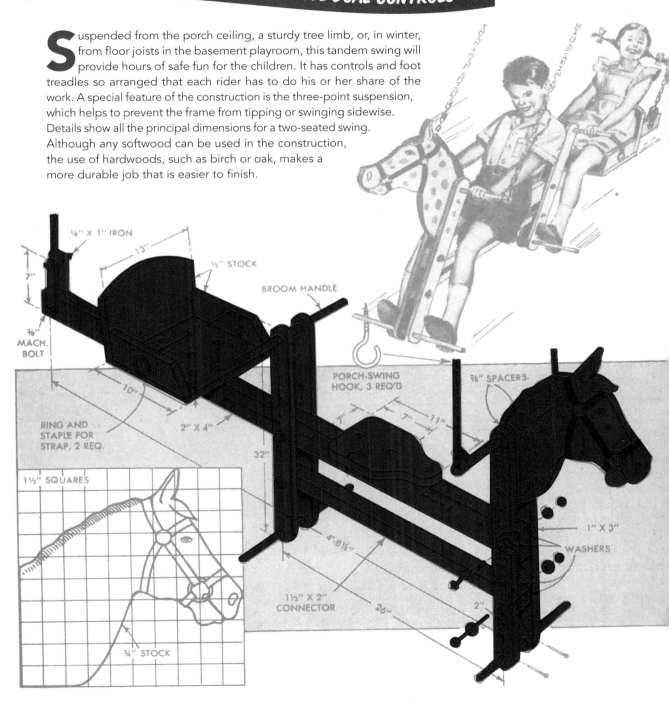

Suspended from the porch ceiling, a sturdy tree limb, or, in winter, from floor joists in the basement playroom, this tandem swing will provide hours of safe fun for the children. It has controls and foot treadles so arranged that each rider has to do his or her share of the work. A special feature of the construction is the three-point suspension, which helps to prevent the frame from tipping or swinging sidewise. Details show all the principal dimensions for a two-seated swing. Although any softwood can be used in the construction, the use of hardwoods, such as birch or oak, makes a more durable job that is easier to finish.

1/8" X 1" IRON

13"

1/2" STOCK

BROOM HANDLE

7"

3/8" MACH. BOLT

10"

PORCH-SWING HOOK, 3 REQ'D

3/8" SPACERS

RING AND STAPLE FOR STRAP, 2 REQ.

2" X 4"

7" 7" 11"

32"

1 1/2" SQUARES

1" X 3"

WASHERS

4'-8 1/2"

1 1/2" X 2" CONNECTOR

26"

2"

3/4" STOCK

Many a farm or country house features a circular swing like the one constructed, which proves very attractive to boys and their friends. The circular swing will be far more popular than the regular version becoming a favorite with all the younger people, boys and girls alike.

To make the one in the illustration, a 10-ft. length of chain was looped around a branch of a large elm, about 18 or 20 ft. from the tree trunk. To the hanging end of this chain, a 1-in. rope nearly 10 ft. longer than was needed to reach the ground was made fast. Directly beneath the point where the chain went around the limb, as determined by a plumb bob, was set a 6-in. piece of cedar post 3 ½ ft. above the ground. Into the top of this post was set a ½-in. rod, to serve as a pivot for the swing. It was set in firmly about 6 in. and projected about 3 in. from the top of the post.

A straight-grained piece of pine board, 15 ft. long, 8 in. wide, and 1 in. thick, was procured and a hole bored in one end large enough to make it turn freely on the pin in the upper end of the post. Two holes were bored in the other end of the board large enough to admit the rope. The first hole was 6 in. from the end, and the second hole, 3 ft. The hanging end of the rope was passed down through one of

these holes and back up through the other, and then made fast to itself about 3 ft. above the board after the board had been adjusted so that it would swing throughout its length at the height of the post, or 1 ½ ft. from the ground. The swing was then complete except for a swivel, which was put in the rope within easy reach of one standing on the board, so that it could be oiled.

One good push would send the board with a boy on the end three or four times about the 90-ft. circle. The little fellows would like to get hold of the board near the post and shove it around. Once started, it could be kept going with very little effort.

In putting up such a swing, make sure to set the post solidly in the ground, because it has a tendency to work loose. Tie all the knots tightly. Do not look upon the swivel as unnecessary. The first swing put up was without one, and the rope twisted off in a few days.

It is not necessary to climb a tree; just throw a stout cord over the limb by means of a stone or nut tied to the end. Then haul the rope and chain up over the limb with the cord. Before the chain leaves the ground, loop the end of it and pass the cord through the loop. The higher the limb from the ground, the better the swing will work, but 25 ft. will be about right.

The circular swing will be found very safe and pleasurable. But, as in the case of an ordinary swing, anyone careless enough to get in the way of it will get badly bumped.

What could be more fun than a swing that doubles as a trapeze? On swings that have chains instead of rope, it is possible to make the swing seat and a trapeze bar interchangeable by removing two links from each chain and inserting a repair link and heavy harness snap at the point the trapeze bar is to be attached. Eyebolts are fitted to the trapeze bar, the ends of the screws being peened so that the nuts cannot come off. The arrangement of fastening the chain to the seat with eyebolts, as shown, can be improved by providing yokes or hangers of an inverted V-shape at the ends of the seat to prevent tipping easily when children stand on it.

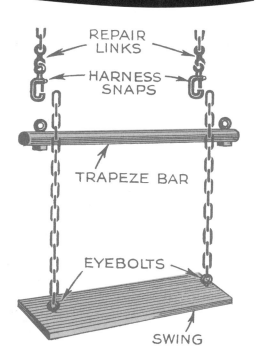

REPAIR LINKS

HARNESS SNAPS

TRAPEZE BAR

EYEBOLTS

SWING

BOLTS

2"X8"

GROUND LEVEL

CREOSOTED

Bolted securely across two 4-by-4-in. vertical members of a child's swing, a 2-in. plank below the ground surface was found highly effective as a substitute for diagonal bracing, which was desired both on account of the possibility of tripping over the braces and because of its appearance. Side pull exerted on the vertical members is distributed over the entire area of the plank, preventing the vertical members from working loose. All wood underground should be creosoted.

CHILD'S HOMEMADE SWING SEAT

A very useful swinging seat for children can be made from a box or packing case. Procure a box of the right size, and saw it out in the shape shown in the illustration. The apron or board in front slides on the two front ropes. The board can be raised to place the child in the box and to remove him. The ropes are fastened to the box by tying knots in their ends and driving staples over them. Always check the ropes for fraying before every use.

TIRE SWING FOR TOTS

Designed for very young children, the modern tire swing shown was made by cutting out a discarded automobile tire and turning it inside out so that the tread formed the seat. It boasts a seat back for safety, plus plenty of places for small hands to hang on tight. Cutting will be a great deal easier if you use a razor-sharp knife that has been heated. Ideally, you should alternate cutting with two knives so that one can be heating while the other is in use. A hot, sharp blade will cut through the heaviest tire, but be careful about overheating, for this can ruin the knife.

HOLES

Children too young for ordinary swings will be safe if the swing is equipped with a seat that will not tip. Box construction and threading of the rope through two holes in each side make this seat particularly safe.

STURDY SWING HANGERS

Made so there is no rubbing where it is fastened to the branch of a tree, this swing is sturdy enough for almost any child. The hangers are two lengths of flat iron that are bolted around the limb with pulleys attached to the hangers. The ropes are run through the sheaves and tied. There should be padding between the flat iron and the branch. Be sure to select a hearty branch that's up for the job.

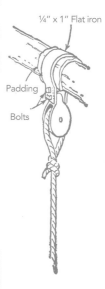

¼" x 1" Flat iron

Padding

Bolts

CHILD'S SWING BUILT OF PIPES IN A NARROW SPACE

A narrow space between two city houses was used to erect a swing as detailed in the illustration. A piece of 2-in. iron pipe, *A*, was cut 1 ft. longer than the space between the walls. Two pieces of 2 ½ in. pipe and a 2 ½-by-2 ½-by-1 ¼-in. tee, as shown in the detail, were slipped over the 2-in. pipe, which was built into the walls. A 1 ¼-in. pipe, *B*, 20 ft. long, bent as shown, was joined to the tee. And a seat, *C*, was attached. The construction of the seat is shown in detail, being fixed to the wooden part with washers, nuts, and a threaded nipple, *D*. A cushion and a removable safety bar, *E*, were also features. This swing is safer than one of rope, and will stand much greater wear.

This substantial swing guards the youngsters from injury brushing against the brick walls.

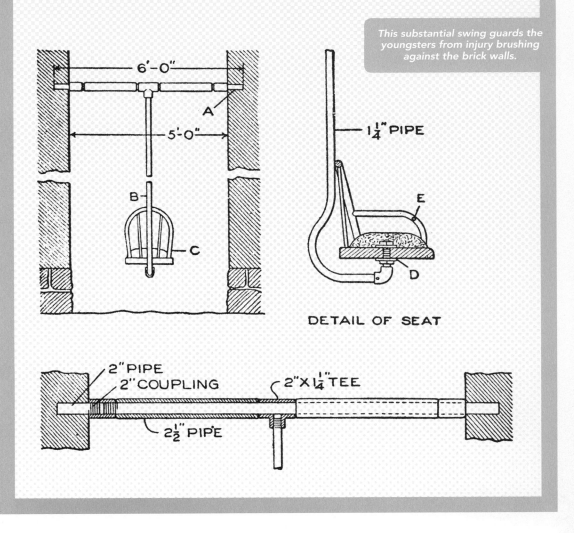

DETAIL OF SEAT

MAKE A PORCH SWING CHAIR

The materials needed for making this porch swing chair are two pieces of round wood 2 ½ in. in diameter and 20 in. long, and two pieces 1 ¼ in. in diameter and 40 in. long. These longer pieces can be made square, but for appearance it is best to have them round or square with corners rounded. A piece of canvas, or other stout cloth, 16 in. wide and 50 in. long, is to be used for the seat. The two short pieces of wood are used for the ends of the chair and two 1-in. holes are bored in each of them, 1 ½ in. from the ends. Between the holes and the ends, grooves are cut around them to make a place to fasten ropes, as shown at B, Figure 1. The two longer pieces are used for the sides, and a tenon is cut on each end of them to fit in the 1-in. holes

bored in the end pieces, as shown at A, Figure 1. The canvas is now tacked on the end pieces and the pieces given one turn before placing the mortising together.

The chair is now hung up to the porch ceiling with ropes attached to a large screw eye or hook. The end of the chair to be used for the lower part is held about 16 in. from the floor with ropes direct from the grooves in the end pieces to the hook. The upper end is supported by using a rope in the form of a loop or bail, as shown in Figure 2. The middle of the loop or bail should be about 15 in. from the end piece of the chair. Another rope is attached to the loop and through the hook and to a slide, as shown. This will allow for adjustment to make the device into a chair or hammock.

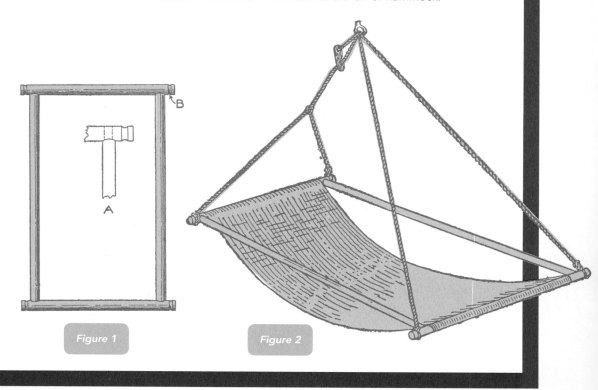

Figure 1

Figure 2

A comfortable porch or lawn swing can be easily and quickly made with a chair as a seat, as follows. Procure some rope of sufficient strength to bear the weight of the person, and fasten one end securely to one of the front legs of the chair and the other end to the same side of the back, as shown in the illustration, allowing enough slack to form a right angle. Another piece of rope of the same length is then attached to the other side of the chair. The supporting ropes are tied to these ropes and to the joist or holding piece overhead.

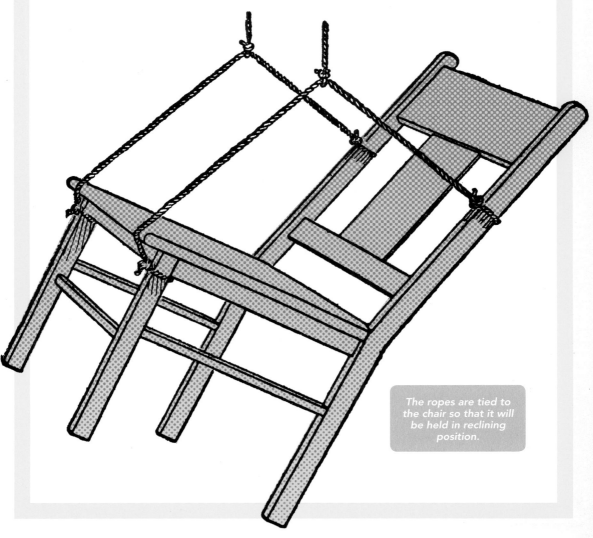

The ropes are tied to the chair so that it will be held in reclining position.

PLAYGROUND AERONAUTICS

SEESAWS NEED NOT ALL BE ALIKE

That's right. They needn't all be alike. They can have considerable variety. Here, for example, are four types, plus as many different kinds of fun.

AERIAL The first one swings on a universal joint; that is, it can go up and down and around at the same time. One lass and a companion each grab an end. The lightweight really gets a ride 'round and 'round and up, too.

HIGH-LIFT Then there's this version. The upgoing passenger may feel as if she's about to take off from a springboard, but that's okay. If she hangs on to the sturdy handles provided, she'll come down again. So will the other youngster when her turn comes. The detail drawing shows how it's made, in a sort of cantilever style. Posts should be anchored firmly in solid ground or concrete.

SOLO These two are designed exclusively for solo flights. On one, as shown right, the dummy passenger is a box of sand. Find the right spot on the long end of the board where nice balance is attained, and away you go. The other number, shown in the detail on the left, performs much like a springboard. Strong coil springs give the bounce necessary to keep things lively. Parts should be amply strong.

LAZY LOUIE This one's still different. Arms instead of legs supply the motive power. Riders about equally matched in weight sit in bucket seats and make with the hand levers. Sections cut from old tire casings and attached to the plank keep the bumps safe and satisfying. Operating this one by hand actually takes a lot more energy, but the riders never know the difference.

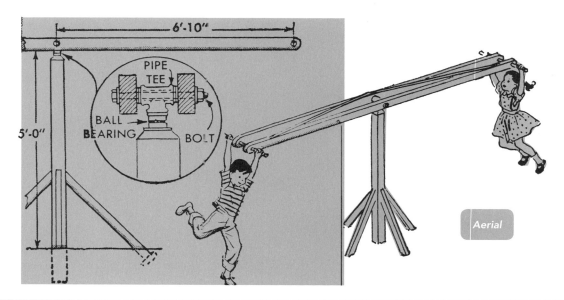

Aerial

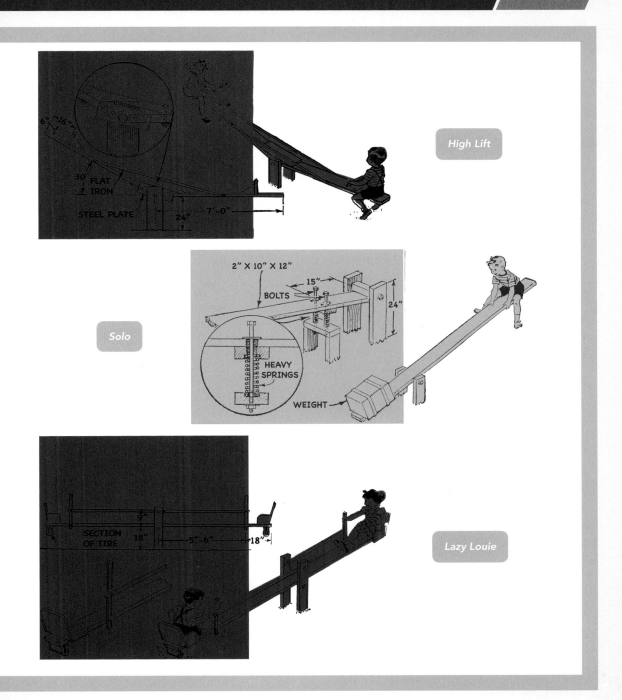

High Lift

6" 16"

30° FLAT IRON

STEEL PLATE

24" 7'-0"

Solo

2" X 10" X 12"

BOLTS

15"

24"

HEAVY SPRINGS

WEIGHT

Lazy Louie

SECTION OF TIRE

9"

18" 5"-6" 18"

GRAVITY-DEFYING RIDES

A single child, seeking means of entertaining herself, has a hard time in getting any pleasure out of the ordinary seesaw.

The drawing shows a combination of seesaw and rocking horse that can be used by one child. The construction is quite simple, the dimensions and weight of the counterweight being varied to meet different requirements. The seat is supported on an iron axle by a pair of strap hinges, one end of each hinge being bent to fit around the axle. The counterweight, which may be an iron casting or a block of cement, is attached to a curved iron rod fastened under the front end of the seat. The counterweight should be a trifle heavier than the combined weight of child and board, and a little experimenting will be necessary to strike the correct balance. The exact mass of weight can be found by first attaching a bucket or bag of sand to the end of the rod, and adding or removing sand until the proper weight has been found.

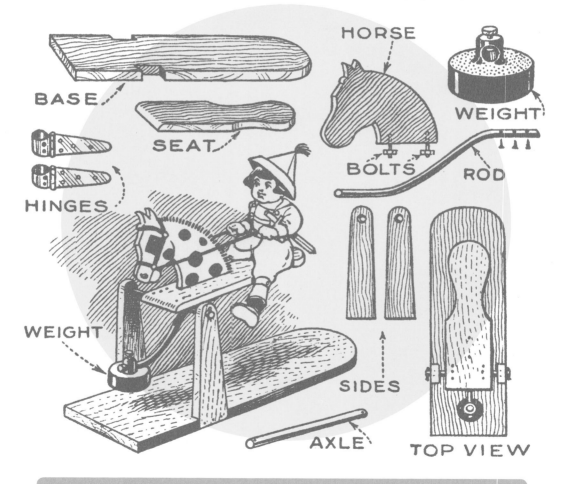

BASE

SEAT

HINGES

WEIGHT

HORSE

WEIGHT

BOLTS

ROD

SIDES

AXLE

TOP VIEW

A combination of rocking horse and seesaw that makes it possible for a lone youngster to entertain herself. A counterweight is provided for balancing the weight of the child and seat.

PORTABLE SEESAW

This seesaw consists merely of a plank balanced on an empty oil drum. To make it, cut two wooden blocks to fit the curvature of the drum and screw them to the plank. Bolt the plank and blocks to the drum, first cutting a hole in one end of the drum to allow tightening the bolts from the inside. A handhold can be made by driving a piece of broomstick into an undersize hole. The safer T-shape handhold may be made from pipe fittings, using a short nipple and tee for the vertical member. This is screwed into a pipe flange attached to the plank. Pipe nipples turned into the tee at the top of the pipe serve as handles.

SPRINGBOARD

To make this springboard, use a fairly flexible hardwood of suitable size. Note that the fixed end is hinged to a garage or other convenient building so that it can be folded up out of the way. Support for the board is provided by a post to which a crosspiece is nailed. Be sure that the post is driven solidly into the ground.

The accompanying sketch shows a playground trolley line that furnished a great deal of amusement to many children at a minimum cost. The wire, which is 3/16 in. in diameter, was stretched between a tree and a barn across a vacant quarter block. The strength of the wire was first tested by a heavy man. When not in use, the wire is unhooked from the tree and hauled into the barn and coiled loosely in the hay loft. The wire was made taut for use by a rope that was fastened to the beams in the barn. The trolley was made, as shown in Figures 1 and 2, of strips of wood bolted with stove bolts on two grooved pulleys. The middle wide board was made of hardwood. The wheels were taken from light pulley blocks and stove bolts were purchased from a local hardware store to accurately fit the hubs. Because it was necessary to keep the bearings greased, we used Vaseline. This coaster made great sport for the youngsters, and at no time were they in danger from a serious fall because the line was hung low and the slant of the wire was moderate.

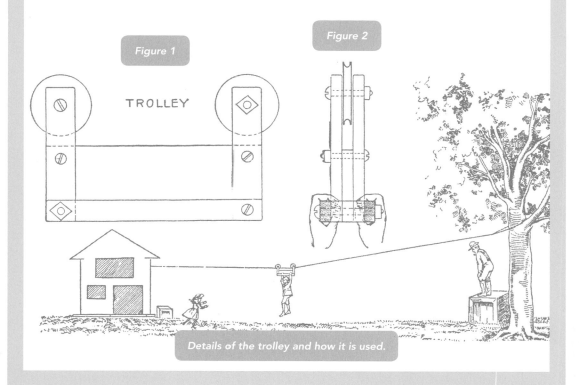

Figure 1

Figure 2

TROLLEY

Details of the trolley and how it is used.

An inexpensive merry-go-round can be made of a single pole set in the ground where there is sufficient vacant space for the turning of the ropes. The pole may be of gas pipe or wood, long enough to extend about 12 ft. above the ground. An iron wheel is attached on the upper end so that it will revolve easily on an axle, which may be an iron pin driven into the post. A few iron washers placed on the pin under the wheel will reduce the friction.

Ropes of varying lengths are tied to the rim of the wheel. The rider takes hold of a rope and runs around the pole to start the wheel in motion. He then swings clear of the ground. Streamers of different colors, and flowers for special occasions, may be attached to make a pretty display.

The ropes tied to the wheel rim will easily turn around the pole.

Step right up! Three twisting thrillers for a penny—a tenth of a dime!" was the familiar invitation that attracted customers to the delights of a homemade merry-go-round of novel design. The patrons were not disappointed, but came back for more. The power for the whirling thriller is produced by the heavy, twisted rope suspended from the limb of a tree or other suitable support. The rope is cranked up by means of a notched disk, A, grasped at the handle, B, the car being lifted off. The thriller is stopped when the brake plate I rests on the weighted box L.

Manila rope, ¾ in. or more in diameter, is used for the support. It is rigged with a spreader about 2 ft. long, at the top, as shown. The disk is built up of wood as detailed, and notches, C, provided for the ropes. The rope is wound up and the car is suspended from it by the hook, which should be strong and deep enough so that the rope cannot slip out, as indicated at H.

The car is made of a section of 2-by-4-in. lumber, D. The lumber should be 10 ft. long, to which braces, E, of 1-by-4-in. lumber are fastened with nails or screws. The upper ends of the pieces E are blocked up with the centerpiece F, nailed securely, and the wire link G is fastened through the joint.

The seats, J, are suspended at the ends of the 2- by 3-in. bar, with their inner ends lower, as shown. This provides better seating when the thriller is in action. The seats are supported by rope or strap-iron brackets, K, set 15 in. apart. The box should be high enough so that the seats do not strike the ground.

The supporting ropes are wound up at the disk A. The car is hooked into place and the passengers take their seats for a thrilling ride, until the brake plate I rests on the box.

Youngsters will get a thrill out of this wind-driven merry-go-round. Mounted on the front wheel and spindle of a car axle, it will rotate even in a breeze because of roller bearings in the wheel. One half of an axle housing is bolted to the wheel to hold chains for supporting the pipe arms, from which the seats are hung and to which dummy boats carrying the sails are attached. The assembly is supported by a pipe set 3 ft. in concrete. The stub end of the axle is inserted into the pipe and held by L-bolts.

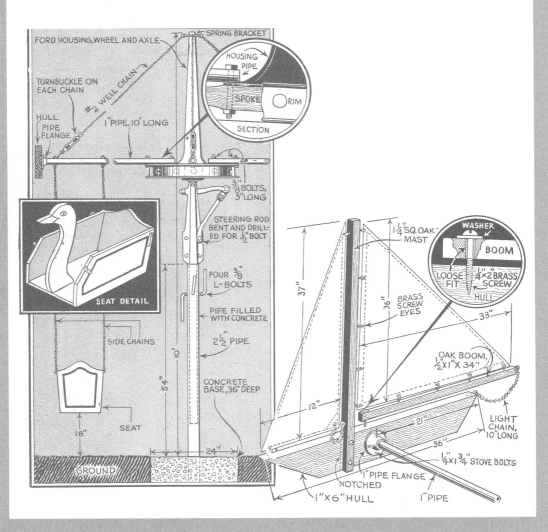

101 THINGS THAT FLY

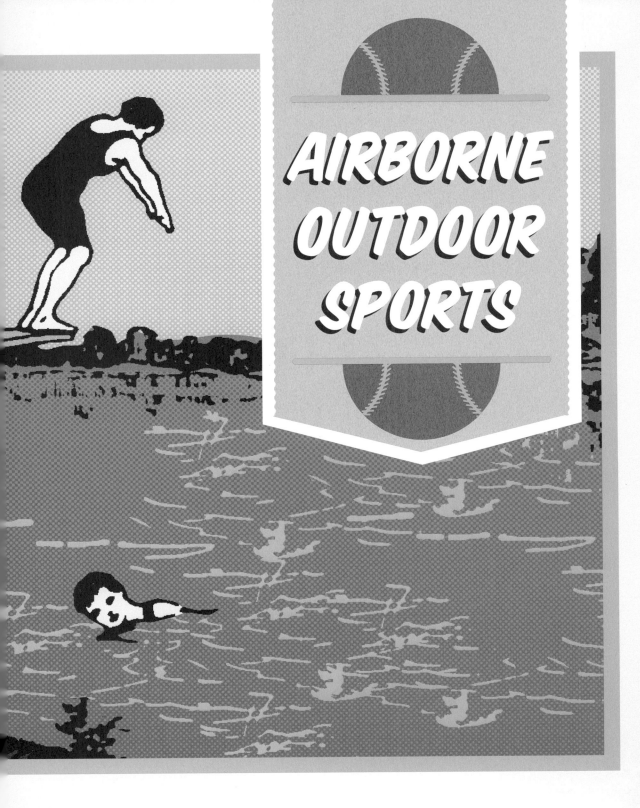

AIRBORNE OUTDOOR SPORTS

HIGH-FLYING AQUATICS

NON-SLIP DIVING BOARD

The slippery surface of a wet diving board is often the cause of injury to swimmers, so the manager of a lake resort devised a very simple and practical method for making the boards at his beach slip-proof. A number of rubber bands, about 2 in. wide, were cut from discarded inner tubes and snapped over the board, spaced about 1 in. apart. Happily, these rubber bands provided enough friction for the divers' feet to prevent them from slipping, even when attempting more complicated dives off the board.

RUBBER BANDS

STONE

DIVING TOWER FOR THE SUMMER CAMP

Aquatic pleasures and sports at a summer camp or lake may be considerably enlivened by the building of a diving tower like that shown in the sketch. It has proved very successful at a summer camp at Crystal Lake, Illinois. The youngsters have made a practice for several years of building a tower early each swimming season on the opening of their camp in July and disposing of it at the close of camp some weeks later. Several resorts and cottages now boast towers made by the campers.

The tower is built largely of 2-by-4-in. stock. The longer pieces at the corners are 12 ft. in length, slanted so that the lower end of the tower is 7 ft. square and the platform at the top 3 ft. square. The handrail at the top is fixed to extensions of the rear uprights.

A springboard is fastened on two horizontal braces near the middle of the tower and is reached by the ladder. The structure is built on the shore and towed out to its position. It is sunk and weighted by the box of stones supported on cross braces.

Children at a summer camp construct a diving tower each summer and dispose of it for the cost of lumber when they break camp. The tower is built largely of 2-by-4-in. stock and is weighted with a box of stones.

Campers on the shores of a lake or river frequently discover to their dismay that the water near the shore is too shallow to permit diving. The answer to this is a floating springboard, such as shown in the drawing. Two logs, about 20 ft. long and 18 in. in diameter, are fastened, about 5 ft. apart, with heavy planks that form the platform. The springboard rests on a heavy wooden crosspiece, and the end underneath is attached to a similar crosspiece. To prevent the springboard from shifting its position, a wooden pin is driven into the front crosspiece on each side of the board. Instead of using one heavy plank for the diving board, two comparatively thin planks may be arranged like the leaves of an elliptic spring, the longer board being on top. A stone anchor prevents the raft from drifting too far from shore.

Springboard mounted on a heavy raft makes diving possible when the water off shore is shallow.

WOODEN PEGS

Make a springboard for the swimming pool or the "old swimming hole" that actually has "spring" to it. This is made by connecting three boards somewhat after the manner in which the leaves of an automobile spring are assembled. In this way, the spring obtained is much greater than that produced by any single board.

The top board is the longest, the next is about 3 ft. shorter, and the lowest one is about 4 ft. shorter than the second. The inner ends of the boards are set flush. All three are fastened together throughout with screws, and at the points illustrated with iron clamps. The clamps should be as unyielding as possible and made with sufficient space between the ends so that the boards can be clamped together tightly. The clamps are fitted into grooves cut on the underside of the bottom and middle boards, but the upper surface is not countersunk.

A highly satisfactory diving springboard made by bolting three planks together.

Anyone seeking a new aquatic diversion will love the thrills and excitement of coasting down an incline and being projected through the air to plunge into the warm water of a summer lake or other outdoor bathing spot. The illustration shows a slide and the toboggan sled for use on it, which were built by a group of young men at a summer resort. Though the slide shown is perhaps more extensive than most boys would care to undertake, the principle involved may be adapted easily to a model one-fourth as long, less than 20 ft. The slide shown was strongly built of 2-by 4-in. material for the framework, 2-by-6-in. planks for the slide

guides, and 2-by-12-in. planks for the roller bearing. Lighter material may be used for the guides and the roller bearing on a smaller slide, but the framework should be of 2-by-2-in. stock.

The high end of the slide illustrated is about 7 ft. from the ground, but a proportionately greater incline is provided because the beach slopes gradually to the water's edge. It is reached by a ladder fixed to a tree, which acts as an end brace for the slide. If no such natural support is available, the end of the slide must be strongly braced on three sides, to ensure safety. It is inadvisable to build the slide unduly high to provide the necessary incline, because this may result

in accidents. A location where the ground is suitable should be selected rather than assume danger or risk.

The end of the slide nearest the water may be given a slight upward turn, so that when the toboggan leaves it the rider is carried upward before striking the water. The hold on the toboggan should be retained when entering the water, because injury may result by failure to clear it in the plunge. With experience, a dive may be made as the toboggan leaves the slide.

The construction of the slide is shown in detail on page 126. The framework of 2-by-4-in. material should be only slightly wider than the guides, and the

Thrills and excitement that will satisfy the swimming enthusiast and provide a new summer diversion at the lake or river may be had from the water toboggan and slide.

CONT

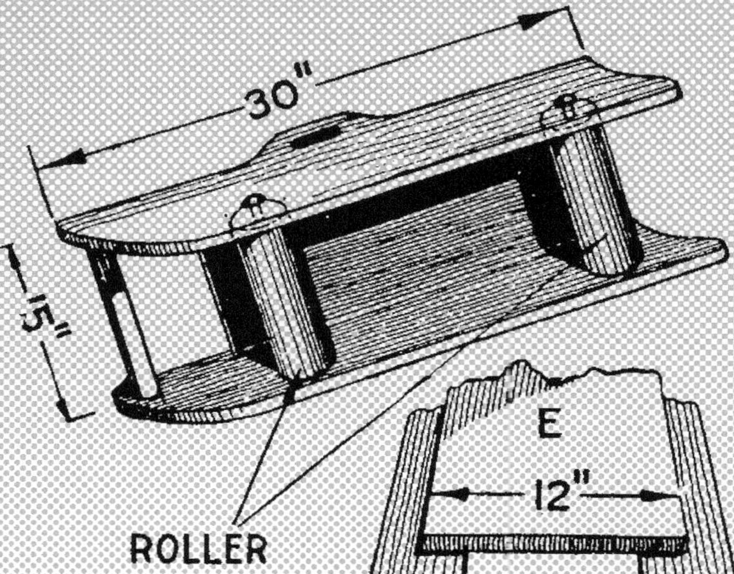

A roller fixed in the side of the toboggan with a bolt and washers.

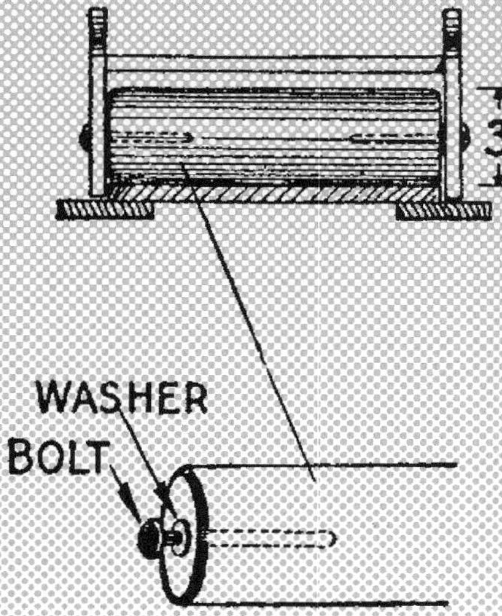

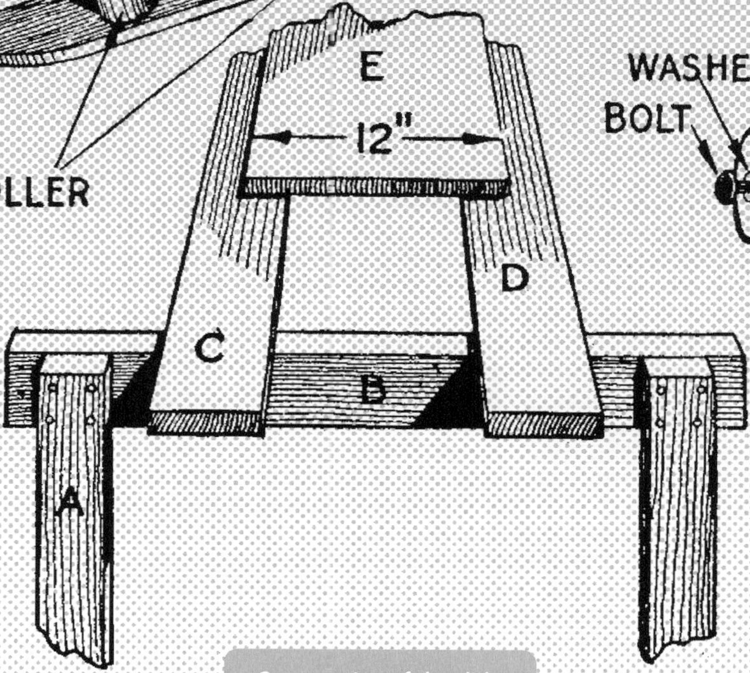

30"

15"

3"

ROLLER

E

12"

WASHER

BOLT

D

C

B

A

Construction of the slide.

101 THINGS THAT FLY

supports should be spread toward the ground to give rigidity. The supports, *A*, should be nailed firmly, or bolted, to the horizontal members, *B*. If lighter stock is used, the pieces at *B* should be nailed in pairs, one on each side of the uprights. The guides *C* and *D* should be of smooth lumber, and the edges of these pieces, as well as of the bearing plank *E*, should be rounded off to remove splinters. The joints in the sections of the guides should be made carefully and placed over the framework supports. They should be reinforced from the lower side by plates of wood.

The bearing plank, *E*, is of 2-in. stock and 12 in. wide. It may be made of lighter material in a smaller slide. The joints in it should likewise be made carefully, to ensure smooth riding over them. They should be set directly over the framework supports, but not on those over which joints have been made in the guides. The plank forming the bearing for the roller should not extend to the end of the slide at the lower end, but should be set back about 18 in. This permits the toboggan to slide off smoothly rather than to spring directly into the air from the bearing on the rollers. The bearing plank may be nailed into place, but care must be taken to set all nails below the surface. A better construction is to use screws or bolts. Bore holes for them through the plank, countersinking their heads.

The toboggan, as shown in the detail sketches, is built strongly. It is to be fitted over the 12-in. bearing plank, allowing ¼-in. play on each side. The sides are of 1 ¼-in. stock and high enough to accommodate the rollers, which should be about 3 in. in diameter. The dimensions of 15 in. in width and 30 in. in length, on the top surface, are suggestive only, and will vary with the materials used. The toboggan will not stand the necessarily hard wear unless good-quality oak or other hardwood is used. The top and foot brace should be fixed strongly with screws, their heads countersunk.

The rollers are fixed in the sides by means of screws, or a bolt may be set through the length of the roller. In either case, the bearing should be in holes bored through the sidepieces. Washers should be fitted at the sides of the bearings, and the latter must be kept greased. All the edges and corners of the toboggan should be rounded off so that there is little possibility of injury from slivers or contact with the edges.

The constantly increasing number of motorboat owners has brought about an equal rise of interest in water sports, among which water skiing is one of the most thrilling. Any craftswoman can make her own water skis at less cost than buying them, and will have the added pleasure of building her own equipment.

Spruce is the first choice of wood for the skis, followed by ash, Port Orford cedar, and yellow cedar. Whatever wood is used, be sure it is vertical-grained so it will take a smooth bend. If you do not have a jointer, have the lumberyard surface and joint the lumber to a finished dimension of 5/8 by 6 in. and square off both ends. The length of the skis should be determined by the weight of the motorboat used. The table at the end of this article will provide this necessary information. While at the lumberyard, get four lengths of 5/8-by-5/8-by-18-in. white oak to be used as the rudders. If oak is not obtainable, the same kind of wood as used for the skis may be used for the rudders. An alternate material for the rudders, depending on personal preference, is 1-by-1-in. aluminum T-bar. The rudders also can be purchased ready-made in some sports stores.

Bending the ski blanks is the first and most difficult step in making the skis, and requires building a bending jig. The jig is built from two 1 x 6s about 6 ft. long. One end of each board is first cut to form the desired radius—20 in. for 5 ft. or less, and 22 in. for 6-ft. skis—and the two 1 x 6s are then joined by cross cleats 14 in. long. The curved section of the jig is either planked solidly with narrow strips, as shown in the detail, or covered with a piece of hardboard to provide a smooth surface.

After the jig is built, the ski blanks must be steamed so they can be bent. The easiest way for the home craftswoman to do this is to set up a 55-gal. oil drum on bricks in the backyard, fill it with water to a depth of 18 in., and build a wood fire under it. The ski blanks are placed in the boiling water and steamed for at least an hour. If the wood is not sufficiently pliable at the end of that time, add more water and boil the blanks longer. When the blanks have been thoroughly steamed, remove them from the water and, holding them side by side, quickly clamp the steamed end over the curved end of the bending jig. Press the opposite ends of the blanks down and hold them with clamps or sandbags. Make sure the straight portion of the skis is parallel to the jig. Use shims and weights or clamps to

The "islands" under the foot bindings of these finished skis are shapes cut from thin stock stained dark.

correct any undesired bends. After the blanks are clamped into place, allow plenty of time to dry and set. One week is the minimum, two weeks are better.

When the blanks are thoroughly dry and set, the next step is to round the front end of each ski. Make a paper pattern, using a 6-in. radius, and then trace the curve on the skis. Cut the curve with a coping, jig, or band saw. Now, sand all surfaces and apply three coats of varnish, allowing plenty of time for drying between coats.

The next step is to install the rudders. If wooden rudders are used, they should be shaped to the dimensions given in the detail, sanded, and varnished. Use three 1-in. No. 6 brass screws to attach each rudder. Holes must be drilled and countersunk in the aluminum rudders to permit installation. The rudders are located 1 in. from the rear end of the skis and ½ in. from the edges of each ski.

Bindings for the feet are next. They also can be purchased ready-made from a sporting-goods store, but the craftswoman can make them from sheet brass or aluminum which is easily cut and worked with woodworking tools. The rubber used is salvaged from truck inner tubes; the runner is extremely tough and is ⅛ in. thick. The half-patterns for the rubber sections of the heel and toe bindings are drawn on ½-in. squares, the paper folded and the completed pattern traced directly on the rubber. The slotted heel plate is drilled and tapped for 10-32 brass machine screws, which are used to hold down the U-shape piece, which, in turn, holds the rubber of the heel binding. Wing nuts are used on the ¼-in. screws which hold the heel plate to permit adjusting the bindings. The strips for holding the toe bindings are drilled

As you rush along in the wake of a couple of husky outboards, water skis give wings to your flying feet.

CONT

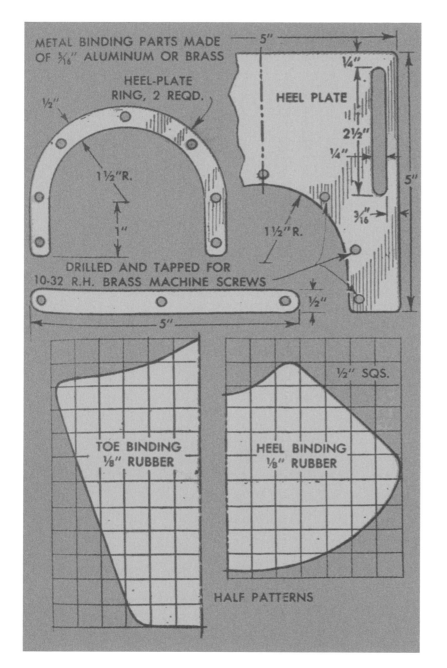

METAL BINDING PARTS MADE OF 3/16" ALUMINUM OR BRASS

HEEL-PLATE RING, 2 REQD.

HEEL PLATE

1/2"

1 1/2"R.

1"

5"

1/4"

2 1/2"

1/4"

3/16"

1 1/2"R.

1/2"

5"

DRILLED AND TAPPED FOR 10-32 R.H. BRASS MACHINE SCREWS

5"

TOE BINDING 1/8" RUBBER

HEEL BINDING 1/8" RUBBER

1/2" SQS.

HALF PATTERNS

The rounded front of the skis is cut with a coping saw after 6-in. radius has been marked from pattern.

After cutting the rounded front end of the skis, carefully sandpaper away all roughness and sharp edges.

Each rudder is fastened 1 in. from back of ski and 1/2 in. from edge. Three 1-in. No. 6 screws are used.

The toe section of the completed foot bindings is fastened with wood screws, the heel with wing nuts.

and countersunk to receive brass wood screws.

When installing the bindings, balance the skis on a thin edge to find the exact center of balance. Locate the bindings so the ball of the foot touches directly on this spot.

The "islands" under the foot bindings are simply ornamental wooden shapes cut from thin stock and stained or varnished a contrasting shade. Figures or designs may be carved or jigsawed and fastened to the islands, as shown in the picture of the completed skis on page 129, to give individuality to your skis. If you do use islands on your skis, find the center of balance after they are in place; it is important that the ball of the foot rests on this balance point so that the skis will ride properly in the water.

After the last coat of varnish is completely dry, all you need to try out the product of your labor is a body of fairly calm water and a friend with a motorboat. Use a good, strong tow rope; one can be purchased at a sporting-goods store. If you haven't been on water skis before, take it easy until you get the hang of it. At 30 m.p.h., the surface of the water is a lot harder than it is when you are swimming.

TABLE TO DETERMINE LENGTH OF SKIS						
Weight of Skier						
	100–120	140	160	180	200	200 +
10 hp.	4½ ft.	5 ft.	5½ ft.	6 ft.	6 ft.	6 ft.
15 hp.	4½ ft.	4½ ft.	4½ ft.	5 ft.	5½ ft.	5½ ft.
15–30 hp.	4½ ft.	4½ ft.	4½ ft.	4½ ft.	5 ft.	5 ft.
inboards	4½ ft.	4½ ft.	4½ ft.	4½ ft.	4½ ft.	4½ ft.

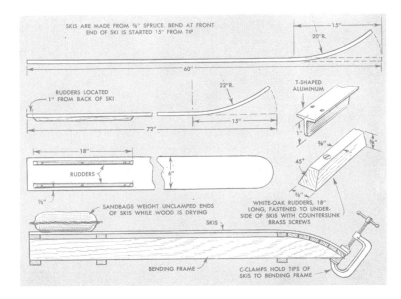

TO PRACTICE BATTING FOR BASEBALL PLAYING

A boy with a very great desire to make a good ballplayer found that he could not hit a ball tossed to him. Try as he might, the bat never hit the ball. Someone suggested that a ball hung by a cord would help to a great extent, and it was tried out with excellent results. An inexpensive ball was suspended from the limb of a tree so that it would be at the proper height for the batter. In striking at the ball, it was not necessary to hit home runs, as this is liable to break the cord, or get it tangled to its support. If the strikes are made properly, the ball will swing out and come back in a perfect curve, or can be made to come back bounding and in no straight line. This will teach the eye to locate the ball and make hits where it cannot be taught by having someone toss the ball to the striker.

THE HORIZONTAL BAR

Gymnastic apparatus costs money and needs to be housed, because it will not stand the weather. Gymnasiums are not always available for the average girl who likes exercise and who would like to learn the tricks on horizontal and parallel bars, horse, and rings, which all young athletes are taught in regular gymnastics courses.

Any small crowd of girls—even two—having a few simple tools, a will to use them, and the small amount of money required to buy the necessary wood, bolts, and rope, can make a first-class gymnasium. If trees are convenient, and someone can swing an axe, the money outlay will be almost nothing. The following plans are for material purchased from a mill, squared and cut to length. To substitute small, straight trees for the squared timbers requires but little change to the plans.

The most important piece of apparatus in the gymnasium is the horizontal bar. Most gymnasiums have two: one adjustable bar for various exercises, and a high bar strictly for gymnastic work. The outdoor gymnasium combines the two. The material required is as follows: 2 pieces of wood, 4 in. square by 9 ½ ft. long; 4 pieces, 2 by 4 in. by 2 ft. long; 4 pieces, 1 by 7 in. by 6 ½ ft. long; 4 filler pieces, ¾ by 3 in. by 3 ft. 9 in. long; and 1 piece, 2 ½ in. square by 5 ft. 7 in. long. This latter piece is for the bar and should be of well-seasoned, straight-grained hickory. It makes no difference what kind of

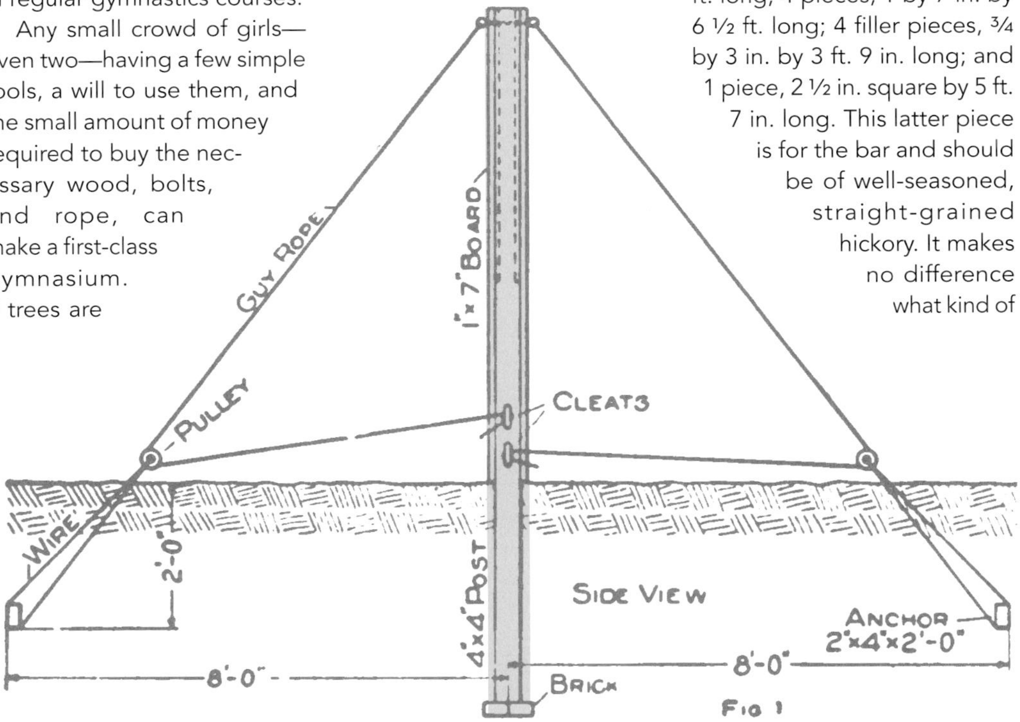

GUY ROPE

1"x 7" BOARD

CLEATS

PULLEY

WIRE

2'-0"

4"x 4" POST

SIDE VIEW

ANCHOR
2"x 4"x 2'-0"

8'-0"

8'-0"

BRICK

FIG 1

Adjustable horizontal bar.

wood is used for the other pieces, but it is best to use cedar for the heavy pieces that are set in the ground, because it will take years for this wood to rot. Ordinary yellow pine will also do very well. The four 7-in. boards should be of some hardwood if possible, such as oak, hickory, maple, chestnut, or ash. The other material necessary consists of 2 bolts, ½ in. in diameter and 7 in. long; 16 screws, 3 in. long; 4 heavy screw eyes with two ½-in. shanks; 50 ft. of heavy galvanized wire; 80 ft. of ¼-in. manila rope, and 4 pulley blocks. Four cleats are also required but these can be made of wood at home.

Draw a line on the four 7-in. boards along the side of each from end to end, 1 ¼ in. from one edge. Beginning at one end of each board, make pencil dots on this line 5 in. apart for a distance of 3 ft. 4 in. Bore holes through the boards on these marks with a ⁹/₁₆-in. bit. Fasten two of these boards on each post with the 3-in. screws, as shown in the top view of the post in *Figure 1*, forming a channel of the edges in which the holes were bored. Two of the filler pieces are fastened in each channel as shown, so as to make the space fit the squared end of the bar snugly. The ends of the boards with the holes should be flush with the top of the post. This will make each pair of holes in the 7-in. boards coincide, so the ½-in. bolt can be put through them and the squared end of the bar.

Select a level place where the apparatus is to be placed and dig two holes 6 ft. apart, each 3 ft. deep, and remove all loose dirt. The ends of the posts not covered with the boards are set in these holes on bricks or small stones. The channels formed by the boards must be set facing each other with the inner surfaces of the posts parallel and 5 ft. 8 in. apart. The holes around the posts are filled with earth and well tamped.

The hickory piece that is to form the bar should be planed, scraped, and sandpapered until it is perfectly smooth and round except for 3 in. at each end. Bore a ⁹/₁₆-in. hole through each square end 1 ¼ in. from the end. The bar may be fastened at any desired height by slipping the ½-in. bolts through the holes bored in both the bar and channel.

Each post must be well braced to keep it rigid while a person is swinging on the bar. Four anchors are placed in the ground at the corners of an imaginary rectangle 9 by 16 ft., in the center of which the posts stand, as shown in *Figure 2*. Each anchor is made of one 2-ft. piece of wood, around the center of which four strands of the heavy galvanized wire are twisted, then buried to a depth of 2 ft., the extending ends of the wires coming up to the surface at an angle.

The heavy screw eyes are turned into the posts at the top and lengths of ropes tied to each. These ropes, or guys, pass through the pulley blocks, which are fastened to the projecting ends of the anchor wire, and return to the posts where they are tied to cleats. Do not tighten the guy ropes without the bar in place, because to do so will strain the posts in the ground. Do not change the elevation of the bar without slacking up on the ropes. It takes but little pull on the guy ropes to make them taut, and once tightened the bar will be rigid.

Oil the bar when it is finished and remove it during the winter. It is wise to oil the wood occasionally during the summer and reverse the bar regularly to prevent its becoming curved. The wood parts should be well painted to protect them from the weather.

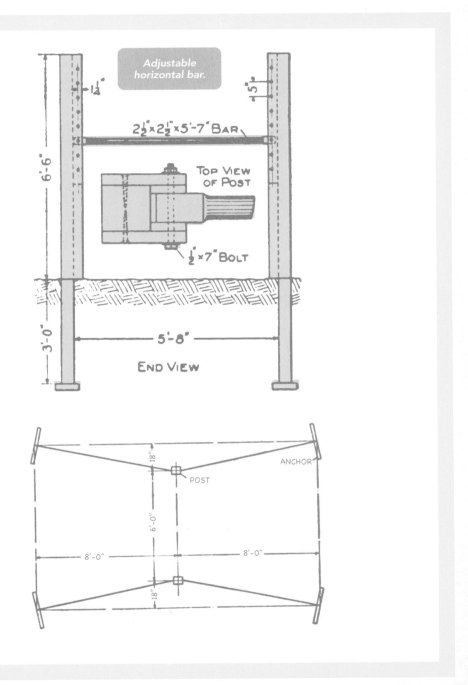

Adjustable horizontal bar.

$2\frac{1}{2}" \times 2\frac{1}{2}" \times 5'\text{-}7"$ BAR

$1\frac{1}{4}"$

$1\frac{1}{2}"$

TOP VIEW OF POST

$\frac{1}{2}" \times 7"$ BOLT

6'-6"

3'-0"

5'-8"

END VIEW

18"

POST

ANCHOR

6'-0"

8'-0"

8'-0"

18"

PARALLEL BARS

Parallel bars hold a high place in the affection of those girls who frequent gymnasiums as the best apparatus for development of the back and shoulder muscles, as well as a promoter of ease and grace of movement. The outdoor gym can have a set of these bars with very little more labor than was required for the horizontal bar.

The materials required are as follows: 4 posts, preferably cedar, 4 in. square and 6 ft. long; 2 base pieces, 4 in. square and 5 ½ ft. long; 2 cross braces, 2 by 4 in. by 7 ft. 8 in. long; 4 knee braces, 2 by 4 in. by 3 ft. 8 in. long; 2 bars of straight-grained hickory, 2 by 3 in. by 10 ft. long; 4 wood screws, 6 in. long; 4 bolts, 8 in. long; 8 bolts, 7 in. long; and 1 dozen large spikes.

To make the apparatus, lay off the bases, as shown in the end view, and bevel the ends at an angle of 50 degrees. Chisel out two notches 4 in. wide and 1 in. deep, beginning at a point 9 in. from either side of the center. These are to receive the lower ends of the posts. Bevel two sides of one end of each post down to the width of the finished bar—a little less than 2 in. Cut notches in these ends to receive the oval bars. Bevel the ends of the knee braces, as shown in the diagram, and fasten the lower ends to the beveled ends of the bases with the spikes. Fasten the upper ends of the knee braces to the uprights with the 8-in. bolts put through the holes bored for that purpose, and countersink the heads. Lay the whole end flat on the ground and make a mark 2 ½ ft. from the bottom of the base up along the posts. Fasten the end braces with their top edges flush with the marks, using four of the 7-in. bolts. Finally, toe-nail the base into the

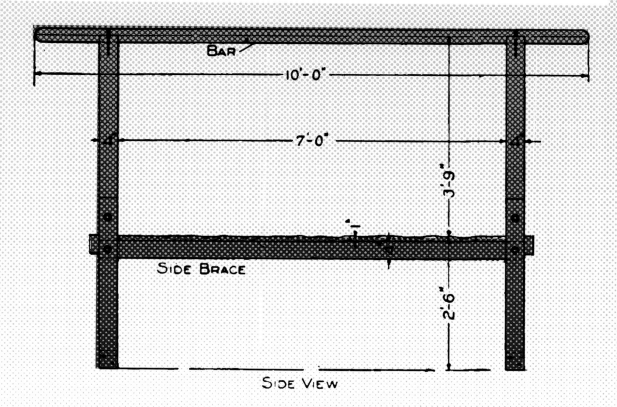

BAR

10'-0"

7'-0"

3'-9"

SIDE BRACE

2'-6"

SIDE VIEW

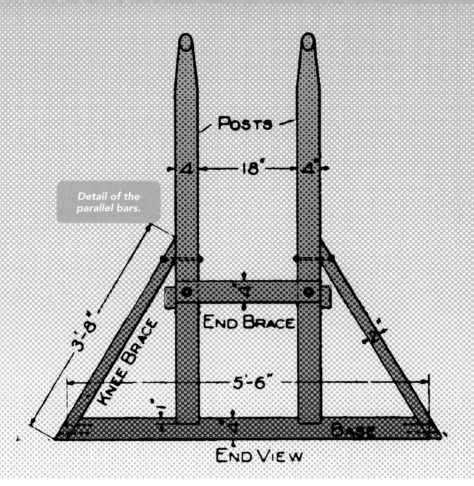

POSTS

4" — 18" — 4"

3'-8"

KNEE BRACE

END BRACE

5'-6"

BASE

END VIEW

ends of the posts merely to hold them in position while the whole structure is being handled.

Two end pieces must be made. These sets or ends of the apparatus are to be buried in trenches dug to the depth of 2 ½ ft., with a distance between the two inner surfaces of the posts, which face each other, of 7 ft. After the trenches are dug, additional long, shallow trenches must be made connecting the posts to receive the side braces. The function of these side braces is to hold both ends together solidly. It is necessary to bury these braces so they will be out of the way of the performer. The side braces are bolted to the posts just below the cross braces, so the bolts in both will not meet. The bars are dressed down so that a cross section is oval, as shown in the end view. They are to be screwed to the notched ends of the uprights with the 6-in. screws. The holes should be countersunk so they can be filled with putty after the screws are in place. The bars should be well oiled with linseed oil to protect them from the weather, and in the winter they should be removed and stored.

Every piece of wood in this apparatus can be round and cut from trees, except the bars. If using mill-cut lumber, leave it undressed. And if using round timber, leave the bark on it as a protection from the weather. It is wise to paint the entire apparatus, save the bars, before burying the lower part of the end pieces. The wood, so treated, will last for years, but even unpainted they are very durable. Be sure to tamp down the earth well about the posts. A smooth piece of ground should be selected on which to erect the apparatus.

The German horse is that peculiar piece of apparatus that is partly a horizontal obstruction to leap over, partly a barrier for jumps, partly a smooth surface of long and narrow dimensions over and about which the body may slide and swing, and partly an artificial back for the purpose of a peculiar style of leap frog.

To make a horse for an outdoor gym, no difficult work is required, save the preparation of the top or body of the horse. The making of the regular gymnasium horse requires a very elaborate woodworking and leather upholstery plant, but the one used for outdoor work can be made of a log of wood. Procure from a saw mill, lumberyard, or from the woods, one half of a tree trunk from a tree 9 to 15 in. in diameter—the larger the better. The length may be anywhere from 4 to 7 ft., but 5 ½ ft. is a good length.

The round part of this log must be planed, scraped, and sanded until it is perfectly smooth, and free from knots, projections, and splinters.

Handholds must be provided next. These are placed 18 in. apart in a center position on the horse. Make two parallel saw cuts 2 in. apart, straight down in the round surface of the horse until each cut is 9 in. long. Chisel out the wood between the cuts, and in the mortises created insert the handholds. Each handhold is made of a 9-in. piece of 2-by-4-in. stud cut rounded on one edge. These are well nailed in place. The body of the horse is to be fastened on top of posts so that it may be adjusted for height. It is not as difficult to make as the horizontal and parallel bars.

The materials required are as follows: Two posts, 4 in. square by 5 ft. long; 2 adjusting pieces, 2 by 4 in. by 3 ft. 3 in. long; 1 cross brace, 2 by 4 in. by 3 ft. long; 2 bases, 4 in. square by 5 ½ ft. long; 4 knee braces, 2 by 4 in. by 3 ft. long; two ½-in. bolts, 9 in. long, to fasten the knee braces at the top; ten ½-in. bolts, 7 in. long, 4 to fasten the knee braces at the bottom, 2 to fasten the cross brace, and 4 to be used in fastening the adjusting pieces to the posts.

To construct, lay out the bases as shown in the drawing, making the mortises to receive the bottom ends of the posts exactly in the center, and cut a slanting mortise 6 in. from each end to receive the ends of the knee braces. Bevel the ends of the knee braces and fasten the upper ends of each pair to the post with one 9-in. bolt. Fasten the lower ends to the base with the 7-in. bolts.

The upper end of each post should have ⅝-in. holes bored through it parallel to the base at intervals of 3 in., beginning 1 in. from the top and extending down its length for 2 ft. 4 ½ in. The adjusting pieces are to be bored in a similar manner after which they are to be mortised into the underside of the horse top 15 in. from each end, and secured with screws put through the top and into the end of the adjusting pieces.

The bases with their posts and knee braces are buried 2 ft. 4 in. in the ground, parallel to each other and the same distance apart as the adjusting pieces are mortised in the horse top. When the ground has been filled in and tamped hard, the cross brace should be bolted in position with its lower edge resting on the ground and connecting the two posts.

The height of the horse from the ground is adjusted by changing the bolts in the different holes connecting the two adjusting pieces with the two posts.

Many pleasant and healthful gymnastic exercises can be had in competitive horse jumping and leaping. The handles provide a way to make many different leaps through, over, and around, including not only those made to see who can go over the horse from a standing or running start at the greatest height, but who can go over at the greatest height when starting from the "toeing off mark"

farthest away from the horse. This horse should be located on level ground having smooth space about it for several feet. Of course, it goes without saying that the horse should be surrounded by a very soft, forgiving surface, such as several inches of firm foam padding, or a pit of equally soft material for landing.

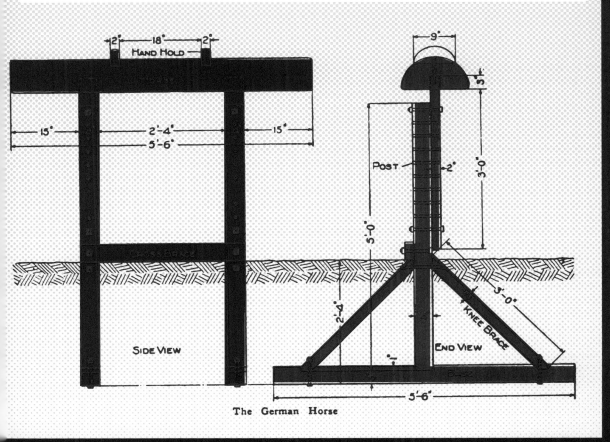

The German Horse

BAMBOO BOW AND ARROW

Almost every girl, at some time or other, would like to try her skill with a bow and arrow, but it can be rather difficult to obtain a satisfactory piece of wood for the bow. Seasoned hickory is usually recommended, but an excellent substitute is bamboo from a cheap fishing pole. With reasonable care and the help of a caring parent, a 5-ft. length of bamboo may be split into pieces of smaller dimensions, twelve or fifteen being obtained from a pole 1 ½ in. in diameter. After splitting it, the pieces of heart or hardened pith at the joints should be removed with a knife or plane so that the strips can be bound together in a compact bundle. The binding is a very particular part of the work, if the bow is to be made serviceable for any considerable length of time. Waxed cord should be used for this purpose. To begin, bind the middle section on the bundle to a distance of 6 in. on either side of the exact center. After fastening the string ends, cut away one-fourth of the number of sticks in the bundle just beyond the wrapping. Bind those remaining at points about 16 in. from the center of the bow. Cut away as many sticks as before and bind again, proceeding in this way until ¼ of the sticks of the bundle remain. These are bound at the tip ends, and the bow is ready to receive the string.

If the work has been done carefully, the result will be a well-balanced bow that will last for years, especially if the bowstring is loosened after using it, so that the bamboo may straighten again and retain its elasticity. Serviceable arrows may also be made of similar material by binding four of the narrow strips together and inserting balancing feathers.

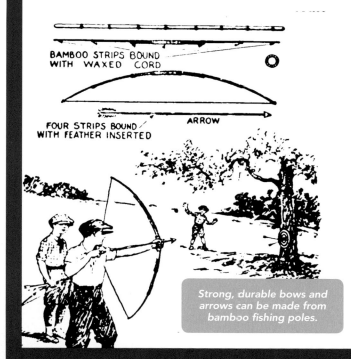

BAMBOO STRIPS BOUND WITH WAXED CORD

FOUR STRIPS BOUND WITH FEATHER INSERTED

ARROW

Strong, durable bows and arrows can be made from bamboo fishing poles.

BOWS

THE LONG BOW: The long bow has a deep or "stacked" body, which is generally recognized as the best type of bow shape. Use a stave of lemonwood for the long bow. Square up the stave to a little over the dimensions at the handle of the weight bow you intend to make. Bandsaw the wood, *Figure 4*, and then round off the belly side with a plane or wood rasp. Cut the nocks 1 in. from each end, *Figure 3*, using a round file, *Figure 2*. Make a bowstring from upholsterer's twine, as shown in *Figure 1*, and brace the bow as in *Figure 6*. When the bow is braced, the height of the string from the center of the bow should be about equal to the width of the hand and thumb with the latter stuck out as in *Figure 28*. You can now "tiller" it to check the bend of both limbs, at the same time measuring the weight with a spring scale, as shown in *Figure 10*.

Bend the bow gradually. Take off a shaving here and there to equalize the bend. Take your time. You can always take off more wood, but you can't put it back on again. The bow should be quite stiff for a distance of about 6 in. at the center, and should then curve evenly to the tips. The beginner's most common fault is to make the bow "whip ended," *Figure 9*. Besides checking the curvature, sight down the bow as you work and note if the string cuts the center of the belly, as in *Figure 7*. If it throws off to the side, your bow has a turn in it. This can be corrected by taking off wood opposite the turn.

If desired, you can back your bow with red or black fiber attached with waterproof glue before the shaping is started. Instead of cutting plain nocks, you may decide to purchase and fit a set of cowhorn tips or you may want to turn them from colorful plastic. It will be noted, *Figure 3*, that plain nocks are not cut across the back of the bow, as this would weaken the wood. The groove in horn or plastic tips, however, is let into the back.

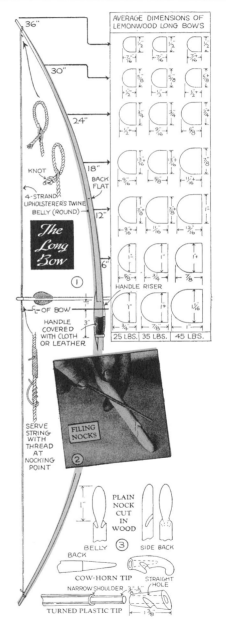

AVERAGE DIMENSIONS OF LEMONWOOD LONG BOWS

HANDLE RISER

25 LBS. 35 LBS. 45 LBS.

36"
30"
24"
18"
12"
6"

KNOT
4-STRAND UPHOLSTERER'S TWINE
BELLY (ROUND)
BACK FLAT

The Long Bow
①

₵ OF BOW
HANDLE COVERED WITH CLOTH OR LEATHER

FILING NOCKS
②

SERVE STRING WITH THREAD AT NOCKING POINT

PLAIN NOCK CUT IN WOOD
BELLY BACK ③ SIDE BACK

COW-HORN TIP
NARROW SHOULDER
STRAIGHT HOLE

TURNED PLASTIC TIP

THE FLAT BOW: The flat bow is easier to make than the long one and can be 3 or 4 in. shorter for the same length arrow. The same general method of bandsawing is used, *Figure 8*, but the belly side is only lightly rounded off. Typical sections of a 40-pound flat bow are given in *Figure 11*. The handle riser can be the same or of contrasting wood to the bow itself. The narrow plate, which prevents wear, is inlaid, using a 5/16-in. disk of 1/8-in. plastic.

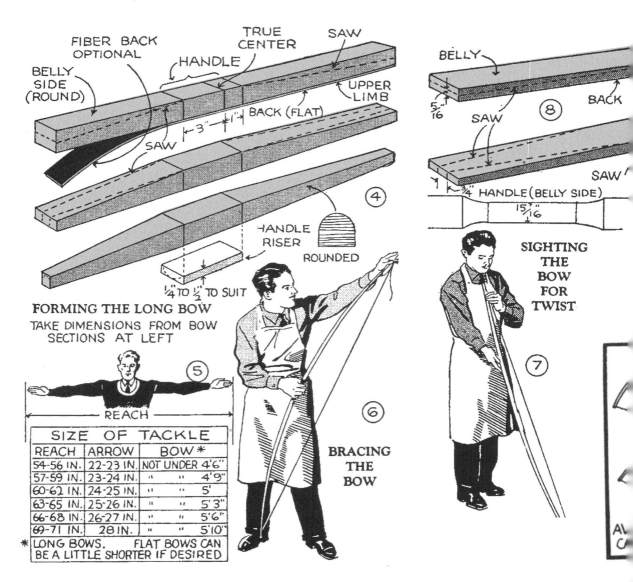

FIBER BACK OPTIONAL

TRUE CENTER

SAW

BELLY SIDE (ROUND)

HANDLE

UPPER LIMB

BACK (FLAT)

SAW

SAW

4

HANDLE RISER

ROUNDED

1/4 TO 1/2 TO SUIT

FORMING THE LONG BOW

TAKE DIMENSIONS FROM BOW SECTIONS AT LEFT

BELLY

5/16

BACK

8

SAW

SAW

1/4 HANDLE (BELLY SIDE)

15/16

SIGHTING THE BOW FOR TWIST

7

6

BRACING THE BOW

5

REACH

SIZE OF TACKLE		
REACH	ARROW	BOW *
54-56 IN.	22-23 IN.	NOT UNDER 4'6"
57-59 IN.	23-24 IN.	" " 4'9"
60-62 IN.	24-25 IN.	" " 5'
63-65 IN.	25-26 IN.	" " 5'3"
66-68 IN.	26-27 IN.	" " 5'6"
69-71 IN.	28 IN.	" " 5'10"

*LONG BOWS. FLAT BOWS CAN BE A LITTLE SHORTER IF DESIRED

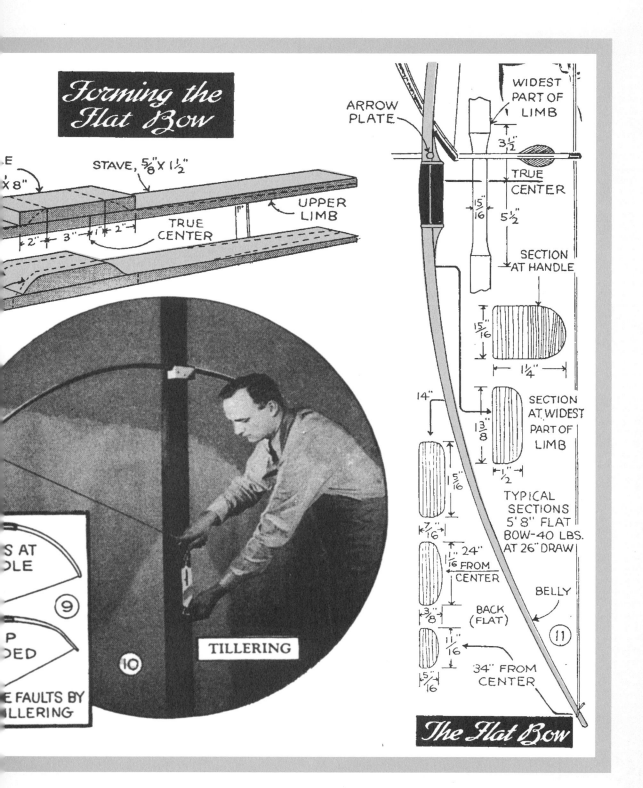

Forming the Flat Bow

STAVE, $\frac{5}{8}$" X $1\frac{1}{2}$"

X 8"

TRUE CENTER

UPPER LIMB

2" 3" 1" 2"

1"

ARROW PLATE

WIDEST PART OF LIMB

$3\frac{1}{2}$"

TRUE CENTER

$\frac{15}{16}$"

$5\frac{1}{2}$"

SECTION AT HANDLE

$\frac{15}{16}$"

$1\frac{1}{4}$"

SECTION AT WIDEST PART OF LIMB

$1\frac{3}{8}$"

$\frac{1}{2}$"

14"

$\frac{5}{16}$"

$\frac{7}{16}$"

24"

$\frac{1}{16}$" FROM CENTER

$\frac{3}{8}$"

$\frac{11}{16}$"

$\frac{5}{16}$"

TYPICAL SECTIONS 5' 8" FLAT BOW—40 LBS. AT 26" DRAW

BELLY

BACK (FLAT)

11

34" FROM CENTER

S AT DLE

9

P DED

E FAULTS BY LLERING

TILLERING

10

The Flat Bow

SELF ARROWS: A "self" arrow is one made from a single piece of wood. The simplest way to make self arrows is to buy a construction kit, which includes the 5/16-in. dowel sticks, feathers, and heads. Birch is the best wood to use. The various parts and dimensions of the arrow are shown in *Figure 12*.

First put on the head. A number of different ones can be purchased, but for average target work, the brass parallel pile head is most satisfactory. Cut the tenon on the end of the shaft by turning on a lathe, *Figure 14*. If you are careful, the head will be a drive fit and will hold securely. If the head is a bit loose, anchor it with a few punch taps, as shown in *Figure 16*. Cut the arrows to the required length and then cut the nocks. Plain nocks can be cut easily by running the

shafts over a circular saw, as in *Figure 13*. The nock should be across the grain. If you want more strength at the nock, insert a thin slip of fiber or plastic. Aluminum or molded-plastic nocks are very attractive and are fitted by tenoning the end of the shaft the same as in fitting the head.

Fletching is the hard part of arrow making. However, if you use one of the jigs shown in *Figures 17 and 19*, you will be able to turn out good work at a fair rate of speed. Turkey feathers can be purchased already cut, or you can strip your own feathers by grasping the vane at the tip and pulling outward, as shown in *Figure 15*, afterward cutting the vane to the required shape.

The one-feather fletching jig shown in *Figures 17 and 18* is built around a paper clip. A disk

of plywood, which slips over the shaft, is drilled with three small holes to supply an indexing head, and is prevented from slipping by means of a piece of spring wire. One feather at a time is clamped by the paper clip and pressed into position.

Any type of adhesive can be used. Celluloid cement has the advantage of quick drying and the ability to anchor on lacquer, thus allowing the shafts to be painted previous to fletching. Waterproof glue on bare wood is the most durable. In the three-feather jig, the feathers are held between metal plates, one plate of each set fitting into grooves in the top and bottom members. The upper ring is removable, being a press fit over the three spacing dowels.

FOOTED ARROWS: Footed arrows are more decorative and

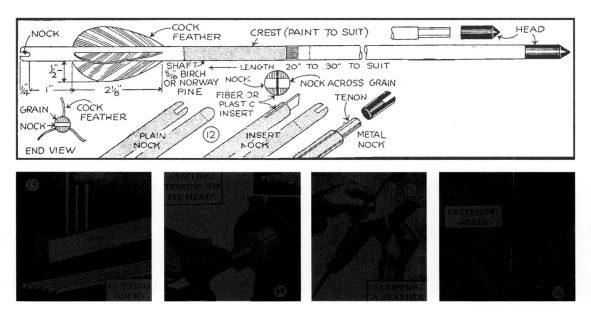

FLETCHING WITH ONE-FEATHER JIG

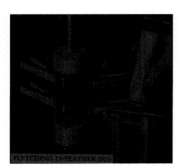

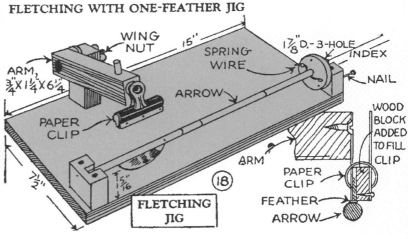

WING NUT

ARM, ¾" X 1¼" X 6¼"

PAPER CLIP

15"

SPRING WIRE

ARROW

1⅞" D. - 3-HOLE

INDEX

NAIL

WOOD BLOCK ADDED TO FILL CLIP

ARM

PAPER CLIP

FEATHER

ARROW

7½"

1⁵⁄₁₆"

18

FLETCHING JIG

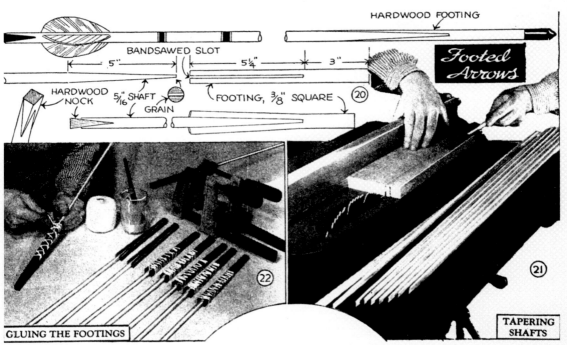

HARDWOOD FOOTING

BANDSAWED SLOT

5"

5¼"

3"

Footed Arrows

HARDWOOD NOCK

⁵⁄₁₆" SHAFT

GRAIN

FOOTING, ⅜" SQUARE

20

GLUING THE FOOTINGS

22

TAPERING SHAFTS

21

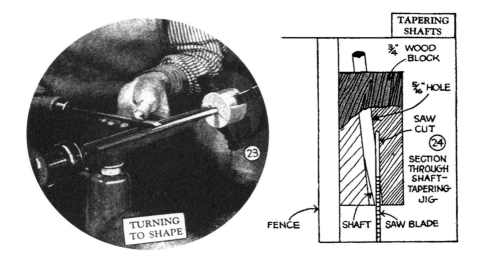

TURNING
TO SHAPE

TAPERING SHAFTS

¾" WOOD BLOCK

5/16" HOLE

SAW CUT

㉔

SECTION THROUGH SHAFT-TAPERING JIG

FENCE — SHAFT — SAW BLADE

more durable than self arrows. The footing is made from any tough hardwood, and is slotted for a distance of 5 ¼ in., *Figure 20*. Shafts are usually Port Orford cedar or Norway pine, and are tapered to fit the slot in the footing. Perfect tapering of the shafts can be done by the circular-saw method shown in *Figures 21* and *24*. The taper should be made with the flat of the grain. The shaft is assembled to the footing with waterproof glue and the assembly is then clamped or wrapped with twin or rubber strips, as in *Figure 22*. Other than

a special tenoning jig, the best method of rounding the footing to match the rest of the shaft is by turning, *Figure 23*. Nocks for footed arrows are usually of the same wood as used for the footing. The insert is let into the end of the shaft, and is later rounded off and grooved in the usual manner.

ACCESSORIES: If you want to be comfortable while shooting, you will need an arm guard and finger protector. Any kind of leather band around the wrist and forearm will do for the guard, its purpose being to take the last of

the bowstring as the arrow is let loose. A simple finger tab of soft leather shaped as shown in *Figure 25* will provide protection for your fingers, or you may prefer to make or buy a three-finger shooting glove. An excellent target can be made by cementing four or five layers of corrugated cardboard together, painting the rings directly on the cardboard or on a piece of oilcloth. A simple target stand is made from ¾-in. lumber, as shown in *Figure 27*.

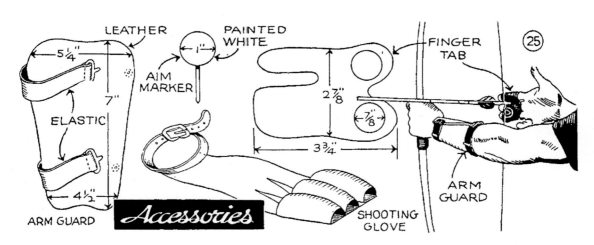

LEATHER

PAINTED WHITE

5 ¼"

7"

ELASTIC

AIM MARKER

1"

FINGER TAB

㉕

2 7/8"

7/8"

3 ¾"

4 ½"

ARM GUARD

Accessories

SHOOTING GLOVE

ARM GUARD

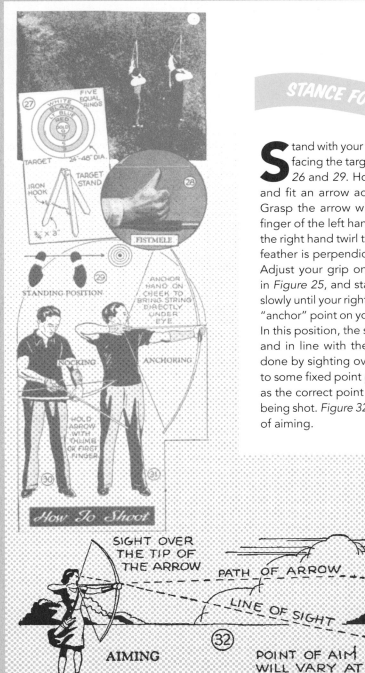

Stand with your feet well apart, left side facing the target, as shown in *Figures 26* and *29*. Hold the bow horizontal and fit an arrow across the arrow plate. Grasp the arrow with the thumb or first finger of the left hand, *Figure 30*, and with the right hand twirl the arrow until the cock feather is perpendicular to the bowstring. Adjust your grip on the string, as shown in *Figure 25*, and start the draw. Pull back slowly until your right hand comes to a fixed "anchor" point on your jawbone, *Figure 31*. In this position, the string should be under and in line with the right eye. Aiming is done by sighting over the tip of the arrow to some fixed point previously determined as the correct point of aim at the distance being shot. *Figure 32* illustrates this method of aiming.

Taped to your archery bow, this adjustable sight will prove to be a more satisfactory method of shooting an arrow than the "point-of-aim" method, because you aim right at the bull's-eye instead of sighting at a marker on the ground in front of the target. Thus, any variation in bowing or in distance is not likely to affect your aim. The parts of the sight are made of heavy sheet-steel or brass, and are cut to the shape and sizes given in the detail. When finished, they should be polished with fine emery cloth or steel wool. Nickel or chromium plating will improve their appearance. The sight is mounted on the back of the bow with the sight end of the cross bar extending to the left. It is adjustable either vertically or horizontally. Once set for a certain shooting distance, the sight may be marked so that when the same distance is shot again, the correct adjustment can be made without any trouble.

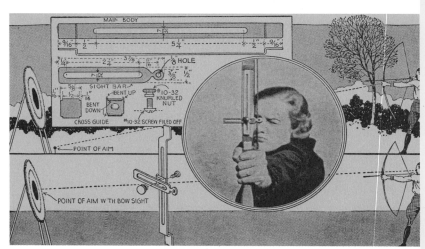

A VERSATILE HOMEMADE BOW SIGHT

This simple, lightweight device has all the adjustable variations of an expensive bow sight. With an average-weight bow, it is fairly accurate for distances well over 100 yards. Cut from a strip of cork gasket material 1 in. wide by 6 in. long, the sight is fastened with adhesive tape to the back of the bow just above the leather grip. After gluing the cork in place, put a strip of tape on the belly of the bow opposite the cork. Stick a 2-in. round-head pin into the cork so that the head projects ½ in. beyond the left edge of the bow. Then, by the trial-and-error method at various distances, determine the proper position of the pin for each distance and mark these positions in ink on the tape, numbering them accordingly. A coat of clear shellac will protect both the cork and the scale.

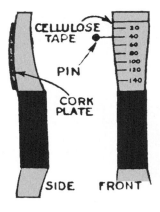

I t is best to use maple for the stock in making this crossbow. But if this wood cannot be procured, good straight-grained pine will do. The material must be 1 ½ in. thick, 6 in. wide, and a trifle over 3 ft. long. The bow is made from straight-grained oak, ash, or hickory, ⅝ in. thick, 1 in. wide, and 3 ft. long. A piece of oak, ⅜ in. thick, 1 ½ in. wide, and 6 ft. long, will be sufficient to make the trigger, spring, and arrows. A piece of tin, some nails, and a good cord will complete the materials necessary to make the crossbow.

The piece of maple or pine selected for the stock must be planed and sandpapered on both sides, then marked and cut as in *Figure 1*. A groove is cut for the arrows in the top straight edge ⅜ in. wide and ⅜ in. deep. The tin is bent and fastened on the wood at the back end of the groove where the rod slips out of the notch; this is to keep the edges from splitting.

A mortise is cut for the bow at a point 9 ½ in. from the end of the stock, and one for the trigger 12 in. from the opposite end, which should be slanting a little as shown by the dotted lines. A spring, *Figure 2*, is made from a good piece of oak and fastened to the stock with two screws. The trigger, *Figure 3*, which is ¼ in. thick, is inserted in the mortise in the position when pulled back, and adjusted so as to raise the spring to the proper height. Then a pin is put through both stock and trigger, having the latter swing quite freely. When the trigger is pulled, it lifts the spring up, which in turn lifts the cord off the tin notch.

The stick for the bow, *Figure 4*, is dressed down from a point ¾ in. on each side of the centerline to ½ in. wide at each end. Notches are cut in the ends for the cord. The bow is not fastened in the stock, it is wrapped with a piece of canvas 1 ½ in. wide on the centerline to make a tight fit in the mortise. A stout cord is now

tied in the notches cut in the ends of the bow, making the cord taut when the wood is straight.

The design of the arrows is shown in *Figure 5*, and they are made with the blades much thinner than the round part.

To shoot the crossbow, pull the cord back and down in the notch, as shown in *Figure 6*, place the arrow in the groove, sight and pull the trigger as in shooting an ordinary gun.

The arrow sling is made from a branch of ash about ½ in. in diameter, the bark removed and a notch cut in one end, as shown in *Figure 7*. A stout cord about 2 ½ ft. long is tied in the notch and a large knot made in the other or loose end. The arrows are practically the same as those used on the crossbow, with the exception of a small notch that is cut in them as shown in *Figure 8*.

To throw the arrow, insert the cord near the knot in the notch of the arrow, then grasping the stick with the right hand and holding the wing of the arrow with the left, as shown in *Figure 9*, throw the arrow with a quick, slinging motion. The arrow may be thrown several hundred feet after a little practice.

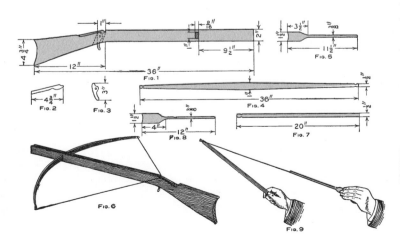

> Details of the bow-gun and arrow sling.

101 THINGS THAT FLY

MAGIC THAT MOVES

THE MAGNETIZED POKER

It has often been said that a black silk thread is "the conjurer's best friend." A great number of tricks can be performed with its aid. One of the most amusing, and at the same time one of the simplest feats is known as the "Magnetized Poker." A black thread is attached to the trouser legs at the knees, the length being suited to the legs of the performer, and varying from 6 to 12 in. long. When the knees are separated, this thread becomes taut. If a poker is leaned against the thread, it will remain in an upright position, kept so by the thread. The performer should make as many passes over the poker as necessary to "magnetize" it before the trick commences, and effective patter is essential for the successful production of this simple feat.

The poker leans against the thread.

THE DANCING HANDKERCHIEF

Another illusion, known as "The Dancing Handkerchief," is also accomplished by means of a thread. The simplest way of performing this is merely to have a black silk thread attached to a handkerchief and running over a pulley in the ceiling. The fundamental objection to this, however, is that nearly everyone at once suspects that a thread is being employed. To offset this and to enable the performer to pass his hands above and below the handkerchief while it is dancing about, he resorts to the following device: A black thread is stretched entirely across the stage; one end of this is attached to a hook about 18 in. from the ground, with the other end in the hand of an assistant. When not in use, this thread is allowed to lie slack, and it will remain on the carpet invisible. The instant it is pulled taut, however, it rises to a height of some 18 in. or more. The handkerchief, which was carelessly thrown over this thread, naturally rises with it, and it dances about in its well-known amusing manner.

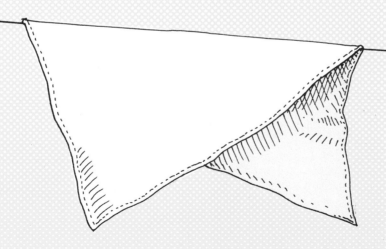

A card is selected—not forced—and then placed back in the deck, which is shuffled and held by a spectator. The performer now requests the loan of a gentleman's handkerchief, which he shows to be an ordinary one. The gentleman holding the pack is now requested to throw it in the air. As the cards descend, the performer waves the handkerchief among them, whereupon the chosen card is seen to be caught on its corner. Both are immediately passed around for inspection.

The following is the explanation of this effective little trick:

On the top vest button, the performer has a small portion of soft, adhesive wax. When the chosen card is returned, the performer places it on top of the pack, which is immediately handed back to the chooser to be shuffled. While placing the chosen card on the top of the pack, the performer quickly and secretly withdraws it, palming it in the hand. As the shuffling of the pack is going on, the performer removes the wax and sticks it to one corner of the palmed card.

A handkerchief is borrowed and held by two diagonal corners, with only the back of the hands being shown to the audience. The corner of the handkerchief is now pressed to the wax on the card, *Figure 1*. The cards are then thrown, and the performer, holding the two corners of the

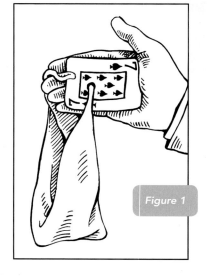

Figure 1

handkerchief between separate fingers, waves it among the falling cards. With a quick flap, he releases the palmed card. The handkerchief shoots out, the card becomes visible attached to its corner, and the effect is that the performer has actually caught one of the falling shower of cards, *Figure 2*.

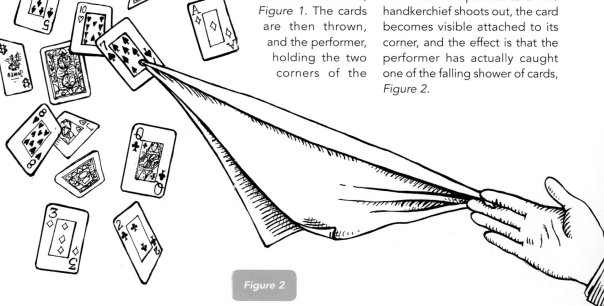

Figure 2

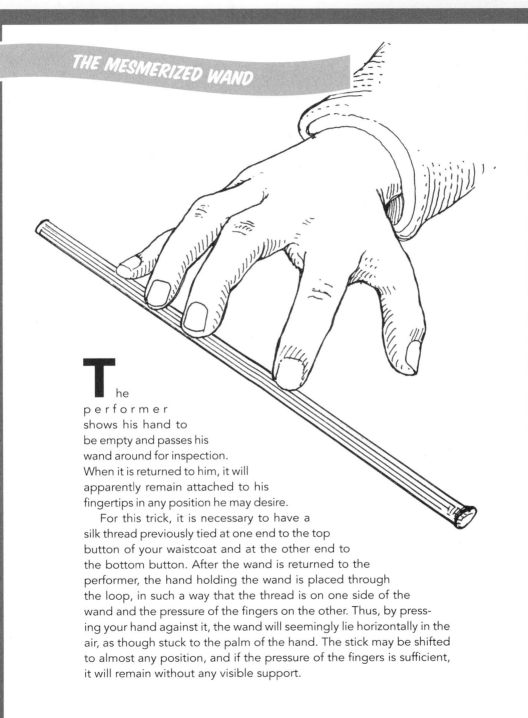

THE MESMERIZED WAND

The performer shows his hand to be empty and passes his wand around for inspection. When it is returned to him, it will apparently remain attached to his fingertips in any position he may desire.

For this trick, it is necessary to have a silk thread previously tied at one end to the top button of your waistcoat and at the other end to the bottom button. After the wand is returned to the performer, the hand holding the wand is placed through the loop, in such a way that the thread is on one side of the wand and the pressure of the fingers on the other. Thus, by pressing your hand against it, the wand will seemingly lie horizontally in the air, as though stuck to the palm of the hand. The stick may be shifted to almost any position, and if the pressure of the fingers is sufficient, it will remain without any visible support.

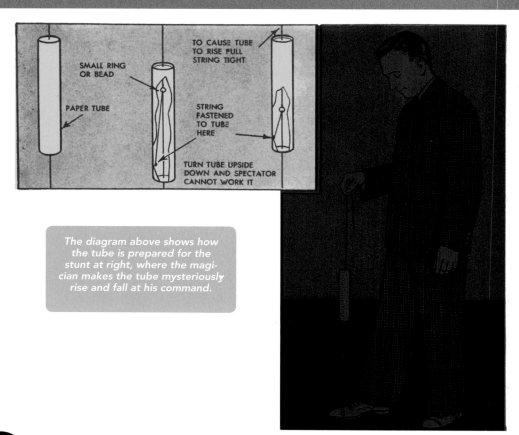

SMALL RING OR BEAD

PAPER TUBE

TO CAUSE TUBE TO RISE PULL STRING TIGHT

STRING FASTENED TO TUBE HERE

TURN TUBE UPSIDE DOWN AND SPECTATOR CANNOT WORK IT

The diagram above shows how the tube is prepared for the stunt at right, where the magician makes the tube mysteriously rise and fall at his command.

THE CONTROLLED TUBE

The controlled tube is a surefire hit. A magician shows a cardboard tube with a string passing through it. Holding one end of the string with his foot, he makes the tube rise or fall on the string at his command. When he hands the tube to someone in the audience, however, and suggests that that person do the same, the latter cannot do so.

Once again, the crux of the trick lies in the manner in which the tube is made. Inside it, about 1 ½ in. from the bottom, glue a small bead or ring. One end of the string is knotted to this, while the other goes through a suspended ring and out the top of the tube. A second string is attached to the suspended ring, the end of which the performer holds. When he wishes the tube to rise, he merely tightens the cord; if the tube is to go down, he keeps the string held limp. In handing the tube to the spectator, the magician turns it upside down. This causes the tube to dangle at the end of the cord, where it can't move.

101 THINGS THAT FLY

THE CLIMBING RING

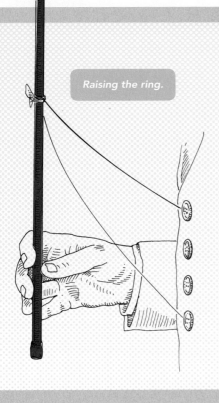

Raising the ring.

The black thread is also responsible for the raising and lowering of a borrowed ring, placed over the magician's wand. The wand has a needle slightly projecting from one end, and over this is slipped a loop of black thread. The other end of the thread is attached to the top button of the performer's waistcoat. A borrowed ring having been slipped over the wand, it naturally carries with it a certain "slack" of the black silk thread. All the performer has to do, therefore, in order to cause the ring to rise upward, is to push the wand (held in an upright position) farther from his body or, with the other hand, depress the slack that exists between his body and the wand. This will cause the ring to rise until it reaches the top of the wand, where it may be removed and at once handed around for inspection.

THE FLOATING HAT

The "Floating Hat" is another illusion produced with the aid of the black thread. A loop some 2 ft. long is passed over the magician's head and neck, hanging in front of him but invisible against his black clothes. A hat, having been borrowed, is dexterously passed through the loop, mouth downward, and the performer, by placing his fingers upon the crown of the hat and pressing downward, is able to raise it and apparently cause it to remain suspended in space, without visible means of support.

THE FLOATING CIGARETTE

The secret of a bewitched cigarette is shown in the illustration. A length of black thread with a pin at one end is wound around the magician's coat button, and pin is stuck on the inside of the coat until the performer is ready to execute the trick. When no one is looking, the pin is pushed into the end of the cigarette, which is then dropped into the bottle. The bottle is moved forward until the thread supports the cigarette; then, moving the bottle back and forth causes the cigarette to rise and fall. This trick should be performed only under dim lights. When the cigarette and bottle are handed around the table, the pin is discreetly pulled out to drop in your lap.

THREAD ATTACHED TO BUTTON

PIN

THREAD

BALANCING FORKS ON A PIN HEAD

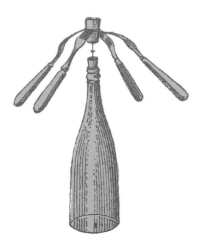

Two, three, or four common table forks can be made to balance on a pinhead as follows: Procure an empty bottle and insert a cork in the neck. Stick a pin in the center of this cork so that the end will be about 1 ½ in. above the top. Procure another cork about 1 in. in diameter by 1 ¾ in. long. The forks are now stuck into the latter cork at equal distances apart, each having the same angle from the cork. A long needle with a good sharp point is run through the cork with the forks and ½ in. of the needle end allowed to project through the lower end.

The point of the needle now may be placed on the pinhead. The forks will balance, and if given a slight push they will appear to dance. Different angles of the forks will produce various feats of balancing.

THE FLOATING KNIFE

Another trick, which is simply an illusion, is shown in the photo. It looks as if the knife is glued to the palm of the hand, but the guests don't see the index finger of the right hand, which holds the knife. To all appearances, the right hand is grasping the left wrist, and one doesn't pause to count the number of fingers visible.

WHAT HOLDS THE KNIFE?

THE EMPTY-GLASS LIFT

BEND STRAW SO THAT IT IS A TRIFLE LARGER THAN DIAMETER OF GLASS

USE BELL SHAPED GLASS

STRAW CAUGHT ON LIP OF GLASS

The next time you are having some refreshments with friends at a soda fountain, tell them you can lift an empty water glass without touching it. All you need is a bell-shaped glass and a soda straw. Before placing the straw inside the glass, bend it so it's a trifle larger than the diameter of the glass. Lift up on the straw lightly, and when the end comes in contact with the lip of the glass, a wedge will be formed sufficiently strong to sustain it. On your first attempt, pick out a landing spot for the glass that's softer than a soda-fountain marble top, in the event that anything goes wrong.

This is a very simple little trick, being merely the passage of an ordinary thimble from the forefinger of one hand to the forefinger of the other, or to some other desired spot. Nevertheless, it may be presented with such variety that it becomes a valuable asset to any conjurer. The first qualification necessary is to become expert in palming the thimble with the thumb muscle, in the fork between the thumb and the rest of the hand. Thus, if the thimble is placed on the forefinger, the latter may be rapidly bent and the thimble deposited in its hiding place in the hand, *Figure 1*. A reverse movement of the finger removes the thimble from the palm and again places it on the tip of the forefinger. This sleight is by no means difficult to acquire, and if performed with the arm in motion, the smaller movement of the finger is quite invisible. The only special precaution to be observed is to keep the hand in which the thimble is palmed with its back toward the audience.

There are many passes and variations that the performer may use, but space confines the description here to but a few. Some magicians begin with the hands in the position shown in *Figure 2*, the right hand having a thimble on the forefinger, and the left a thimble palmed in the fork of the thumb. The performer waves the right hand backward and forward alternately before and behind the other. As the fingers of the right hand vanish behind those of the left, he palms the visible thimble as described. At the same moment, the forefinger of the left hand is bent and the thimble appears on it, the effect for the spectators being that it has flown from one forefinger to the other.

A very good effect is to make the thimble presumably disappear through one part of the body and come out at another. Thus, the forefinger with the thimble on it may be put into the mouth, withdrawn with the thimble absent, and again produced from behind the head with the thimble in its place. Again, the thimble may apparently be put in one ear, then recovered from the other, and other passes of similar effect may be arranged by the amateur. When they are performed with ease and finish, they are both striking and amusing.

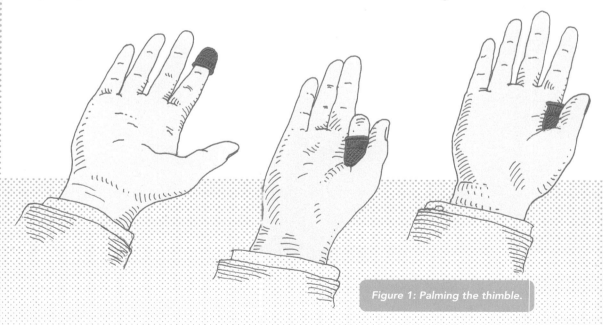

Figure 1: Palming the thimble.

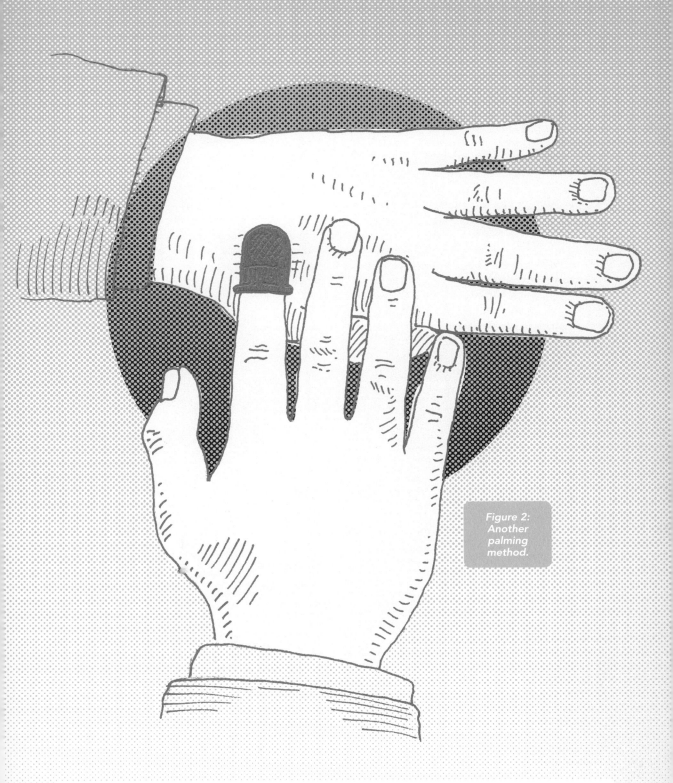

Figure 2:
Another palming
method.

This delightful novelty has puzzled many wise heads in the conjuring fraternity. The magician requests that two or three cards be chosen, which are returned to the pack and shuffled (with a pass and false shuffle). He then explains that, under certain conditions, it is possible to generate enough "magnetic influence" in the tip of his forefinger to "magnetize" a card. Suiting the action to the word, the conjurer rubs his forefingers together, then requests the name of the first chosen card, which, let us suppose, is the 2 of clubs.

The pack is now held by its lower end, between the left thumb and fingers. The magician's right forefinger, held in the position of pointing, is placed about 1 in. above the pack. Slowly he raises it two or three times, without success. But the third time, the chosen card follows his finger out of the pack! This is repeated with the second card, and finally with the third. When the last card is halfway out of the pack, the conjurer removes his hand, and the card slowly sinks back into the pack. The magician explains that this is because the "magnetism" was broken when his hand was removed. The cards are then passed around for examination.

Consulting the accompanying illustration will make the solution clear: the extended little finger carries up the card. The illusion may be added to greatly by failing in the first two or three attempts. The latter part of the trick—that is, the descent of the card—is accomplished by a slight relaxation by the fingers and thumb of the left hand, which can easily be acquired after a few moments' practice.

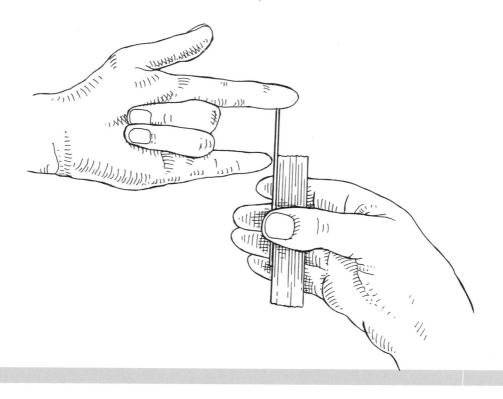

THE SHOWER OF SWEETS

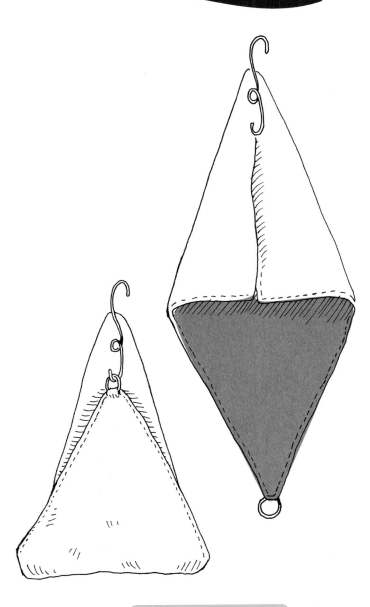

Unhook the flap to release the shower of sweets.

The following is a very anti-quated trick, but one that is always hailed with acclaim from the juvenile portion of the audience. The performer borrows a handkerchief and spreads it on his table. He then lifts it by nipping it between his forefinger and thumb. A lady is asked to breathe on it, and a perfect shower of small candies and sweet-meats falls on a plate held underneath to catch them.

The secret lies in the use of a small bag of muslin or calico, made of the shape shown in the illustration. When filled, it is closed by holding down the flap and hooking the little ring over the hook as shown. When it is time to open it, the hook is slightly tilted forward and the lower flap falls down, thus allowing its contents to shower down onto a plate held to receive them.

The bag is hooked onto the back of the table. In the act of picking up the handkerchief, the little hook at the top is grasped through the handkerchief and the bag is drawn, by means of the hook, up into the sheltering folds of the handkerchief. A plate is then held beneath, a lady is asked to breathe on it, and the "shower of sweets" descends. While walking behind the table to hand the plate of sweets to the audience, the per-former quickly drops the bag onto the servante, and the handkerchief is returned.

THE MYSTIC CLIMBING RING

The performer hands out a wand for examination and borrows a finger ring. He holds the wand in his hand, point upward, and drops the ring on it. Then he makes hypnotizing passes over the wand with the other hand, and causes the ring to climb toward the top, stop at any place desired, pass backward, and at last fall from the wand. The wand and ring are examined again by the audience.

To produce this little trick, the performer must first provide himself with a round, black stick, about 14 in. long, a piece of No. 60 black cotton thread, about 18 in. long, and a small bit of beeswax. Tie one end of the thread to the top button on the coat, and to the free end stick the beeswax, which is stuck to the lower button until ready for the trick.

After the wand is returned, secretly stick the waxed end to the top of the wand, and then drop the ring on it. Moving the wand slightly from oneself will cause the ring to move upward, and relaxing it causes the ring to fall. In the final stage, remove the thread and hand out the wand for examination.

A FLASHLIGHT TELEGRAPH ON A KITE LINE

An ordinary pocket flash lamp is prepared in the following manner: A brass spring, as shown in the sketch, is bound tightly to the flash lamp with a cord. Two wires, one at each end, are twisted around the lamp's body, forming two loops at the top. The kite string is run through the loops and over the spring. The lamp is then placed near the kite. The ordinary pull on the kite string does not close the spring, but a sharp jerk will pull the string in contact with the push button and its slight pressure causes an instant flash of the light. By this method, words may be spelled out in the telegraph code.

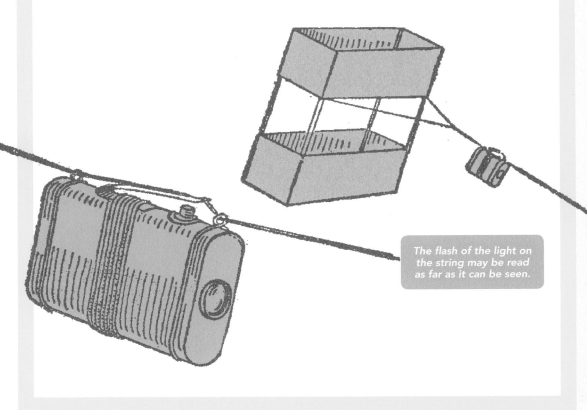

The flash of the light on the string may be read as far as it can be seen.

The heliograph as it is used by neighboring boys to send messages on a clear day by flashing the sun's rays from one to the other. The messages can be read as far as the eye can see the light.

How To MAKE A HELIOGRAPH

The heliograph used in the army provides a good method of sending messages using the reflection of the sun's rays. There are stations in the mountains from which messages are sent by the heliograph for great distances, and guides carry them for use in case of trouble or accident. The wireless telegraph delivers messages by electricity through the air, but the heliograph sends them by flashes of light.

The main part of the instrument is the mirror, which should be about 4 in. square, set in a wood frame and swung on trunnions made of two square-head bolts, each ¼ in. in diameter and 1 in. long. These bolts are firmly held to the frame with brass strips, ½ in. wide and 3 in. long. The strips are drilled in their centers to admit the bolts, and then drilled at each end for the screw that fastens them to the frame. This construction is

clearly shown in *Figure 1*.

A hole is cut in the center of the frame backing and a small hole, not over ⅛ in. in diameter, is scratched through the silvering on the glass. If the trunnions are centered properly, the small hole should be exactly in line with them and in the center.

A U-shaped support is made of wood strips, ⅜ in. thick and 1 in. wide, the length of the uprights being 3½ in. and the crosspiece connecting their lower ends a trifle longer than the width of the frame. These are put together, as shown in *Figure 2*, with small brackets at the corners. A slot, ½ in. deep and ¼ in. wide, is cut into the upper end of each upright to receive the trunnions on the mirror frame. Nuts are tightly turned on the bolt ends to clamp the standard tops against the brass strips on the mirror frame. The cross strip at the bottom is clamped to the

base with a bolt, 1½ in. long. The hole for this bolt should be exactly below the peephole in the mirror and run through one end of the baseboard, which is ¾ in. thick, 2 in. wide, and 10 in. long.

At the opposite end of the base, place a sighting rod, which is made as follows: The rod is ½ in. in diameter and 8 in. long. The upper end is fitted with a piece of thick, white cardboard, cut ¼ in. in diameter and having a projecting shank 1 in. long, as shown in *Figure 3*. The rod is placed in a ½-in. hole bored in the end of the baseboard, as shown in *Figure 2*. To keep the rod from slipping through the hole, a setscrew is made of a small bolt with the nut set in the edge of the baseboard as shown in *Figure 4*.

The tripod head is formed of a wood disk, 5 in. in diameter, with a hole in the center, and three small blocks of wood, 1 in. square and 2 in. long, nailed to the underside, as shown in *Figure 5*. The tripod legs are made of light strips of wood, ⅜ in. thick, 1 in. wide, and 5 ft. long. Two of these strips, nailed securely together to within 20 in. of the top, constitute one leg. The upper unnailed ends are spread to slip over the blocks on the tripod top. These ends are bored to loosely fit over the headless nails driven partway into the block ends. One tripod leg is shown in *Figure 6*.

The screen, or shutter, is mounted on a separate tripod and is shown in *Figure 7*. Cut out two slats from hardwood, ⅜ in. thick, 2 ½ in. wide, and 6 in. long, and taper both edges of these slats down to ³⁄₁₆ in. Small nails are driven into the ends of the slats and the heads are filed off so that the projecting ends will form trunnions on which the slats will turn. Make a frame of wood pieces, ¾ in. thick and 2 ½ in. wide, the opening in the frame being 6 in. square. Before nailing the frame together, bore holes in the side uprights for the trunnions

of the slats to turn in. These holes are 1 ¾ in. apart. The frame is then nailed together and also nailed to the tripod top. The shutter is operated with a key very similar to a telegraph key. The construction of this key is shown in *Figure 7*. A part of a spool is fastened to a stick that is pivoted on the opposite side of the frame. The key is connected to the slats in the frame with a bar and rod, to which a coil spring is attached, as shown in *Figure 8*. *Figure 9* shows the positions of the tripods when the instrument is set to flash the sunlight through the shutter. The regular telegraph code is used in flashing the light.

To set the instrument, first turn the cardboard disk down to uncover the point of the sight rod, then sight through the hole in the

mirror and adjust the sight rod so that the tip end comes squarely in line with the receiving station. When the instrument is properly sighted, the shutter is set up directly in front of it and the cardboard disk is turned up to cover the end of the sight rod. The mirror is then turned so that it reflects a beam of light with a small shadow spot showing the center made by the peephole in the mirror, which is directed to fall on the center of the cardboard sighting disk. It will be quite easy to direct this shadow spot to the disk by holding a sheet of paper 6 or 8 in. in front of the mirror and following the spot on the paper until it reaches the disk. The flashes are made by manipulating the key operating the shutter in the same manner as a telegraph key.

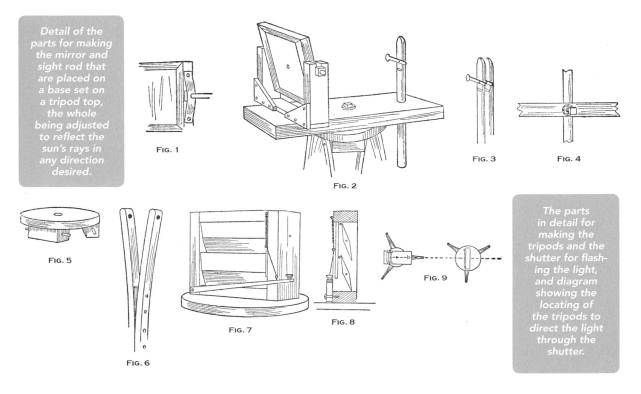

Detail of the parts for making the mirror and sight rod that are placed on a base set on a tripod top, the whole being adjusted to reflect the sun's rays in any direction desired.

FIG. 1

FIG. 2

FIG. 3

FIG. 4

FIG. 5

FIG. 6

FIG. 7

FIG. 8

FIG. 9

The parts in detail for making the tripods and the shutter for flashing the light, and diagram showing the locating of the tripods to direct the light through the shutter.

FEAT OF BALANCING ON CHAIRS

Among the numerous experiments of gravity is the feat of balancing on the two rear legs of a chair while one foot rests on the front part of the seat and the other on the back of the chair. This may appear to be a hard thing to do, yet with a little practice it may be accomplished. This is an exercise practiced by the boys of a boys' home for an annual display given by them. A dozen of the boys will mount chairs at the same time and keep them in balance at the word of a commanding officer.

CENTER OF GRAVITY EXPERIMENT

This experiment consists of suspending a pail of water from a stick placed upon a table, as shown in the accompanying sketch. In order to accomplish this experiment, which seems impossible, it is necessary to place a stick, A, of sufficient length, between the end of the stick on the table and the bottom of the pail. This makes the center of gravity somewhere near the middle of the stick on the table, thus holding the pail as shown.

A man pulling with a force of 100 lbs. can lift only that amount with a single block, as shown in *Figure 1*, but by using two single blocks, he can lift double that amount, as indicated in *Figure 2*. By using a double block above and a single block below, as shown in *Figure 3*, a 100 lb. pull on the rope will lift 300 lbs., and by using two double blocks, as indicated in *Figure 4*, 100 lbs. will lift 400 lbs.

In *Figure 1*, the load is supported directly by one rope; in *Figure 2*, by two ropes; in *Figure 3*, by three ropes; and in *Figure 4*, by four ropes. The weight is 100, 200, 300, and 400 lbs. respectively. Thus, with pulley blocks arranged in this way, the weight that can be raised is in direct proportion to the number of ropes that support it. In these calculations, the portion of rope that the man holds is ignored, as he pulls in a direction opposite to the movement of the weight, but should he take his position above the pulleys and pull up, then the rope that he holds should be counted also.

Another system of arranging pulleys is shown in *Figures 5, 6, 7,* and *8*, the pulley blocks being all single. In an arrangement of this kind, the power is just doubled by the addition of each pulley, as indicated by the figures. In all these calculations, no allowance has been made for friction so that the actual force required to lift the given weights will be somewhat greater, the exact amount depending on the flexibility of the rope, diameter of the pulleys, smoothness of the bearings, and other conditions.

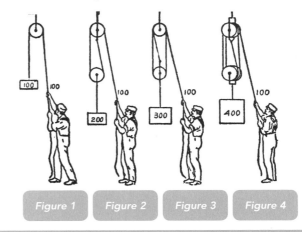

| Figure 1 | Figure 2 | Figure 3 | Figure 4 |

Various arrangements of pulley blocks showing lifting power.

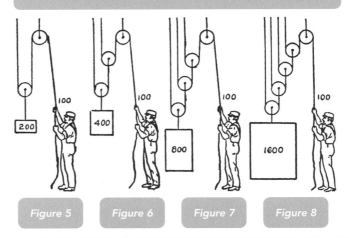

| Figure 5 | Figure 6 | Figure 7 | Figure 8 |

INDEX